D1047334

GROUP THERAPY WITH CHILDREN AND ADOLESCENTS
A Treatment Manual

GROUP THERAPY WITH CHILDREN AND ADOLESCENTS
A Treatment Manual

Edited by
**Barbara B. Siepker, A.M. and
Christine S. Kandaras, A.M.**
with contributions from
**Laura H. Lewis, Ph.D.
Anita K. Lampel, Ph.D.
Charles H. Herndon, M.S.
Margot Schnitzer de Neuhaus, A.M.**

HUMAN SCIENCES PRESS, INC.
**72 FIFTH AVENUE,
NEW YORK, N.Y. 10011**

Printed in the United States of America
987654321

Library of Congress Cataloging in Publication Data

Main entry under title:

Group therapy with children and adolescents.

Includes index.
1. Group psychotherapy. 2. Child psychotherapy.
3. Adolescent psychotherapy. I. Siepker, Barbara B.
II. Kandaras, Christine S. [DNLM: 1. Psychotherapy,
Group—in adolescence. 2. Psychotherapy, Group—in
infancy & childhood. WS 350.2 G8825]
RJ505.G7G77   1985   618.92'89152   84-27845
ISBN 0-89885-242-0

618.9289152
G9183
Cop 2

Edu.

CONTENTS

DEDICATION

This book is dedicated to all those who have survived and enjoyed group therapy with children and adolescents; but most especially it is dedicated, with love and respect, to all those children who have borne with us while we learned and in the process have shared themselves with us. It would not have been possible, though, without the love and sharing of those closest to us. We thank you all for your patience, understanding, and sharing.

PREFACE

This book emerged from the authors' struggles to develop a seminar on group psychotherapy with children and adolescents for our colleagues and trainees in the Division of Child Psychiatry at The Children's Memorial Hospital, a private, nonprofit hospital on the north side of Chicago. The hospital offers comprehensive medical, surgical, and psychiatric services to children from birth through sixteen years of age; additionally, it is the pediatric training hospital for McGaw Medical Center of Northwestern University. The patient population is composed of a diverse cultural and socioeconomic group. A large multidisciplinary staff provides comprehensive mental health care to children and their families. The division's approach is eclectic, and we struggled to keep it that way in our presentation.

Pulling together our varied experiences, training, theoretical orientations, and the literature into a thorough, worthwhile presentation for clinicians quickly impressed us with the immensity of the undertaking. As we progressed, we made several discoveries. The literature available did not speak to the difficulties, thoughts, and feelings experienced by the therapist throughout his or her contact with a group of emotionally disturbed children. We soon saw that in order to answer the questions we asked ourselves and were being asked we needed to describe the observable experiences in the group, explain them dynamically, and integrate the two. Additionally, special issues and techniques needed thorough discussion. Another discovery was that the authors' practical approaches to group psychotherapy were very similar even though we had a diversity of training and professional backgrounds. Discussing our experiences, we found that in addition there were similarities both in the paths pursued by the groups and in the affective experiences of the children and the therapist. These discoveries shaped our approach to our task and led naturally into the structure and format of this book.

We would like gratefully to acknowledge the inspiration and support of the teachers and colleagues with whom we have worked during our training, practice, and teaching. We appreciated the many opportunities to share ideas and to listen to valuable feedback, especially from our readers, Dr. Jerome L. Schulman, head of the Division of Child Psychiatry, and Dr. Mary Louise Somers, Professor Emeritus, School of Social Service Administration of the University of Chicago. The first version was compiled under the direction of Mrs. Roberta Woods of the division's clerical services. Chapter 2 was read by Dr. E. J. Anthony, Margaret G. Frank, and Dr. Hyman L. Muslin.

Chapter 1

RELATIONSHIP-ORIENTED GROUP PSYCHOTHERAPY WITH CHILDREN AND ADOLESCENTS

Barbara B. Siepker,
Laura H. Lewis,
Christine S. Kandaras

This book proposes a developmental model of group psycho-therapy with children and adolescents that emphasizes relation-ships in the therapeutic process. Most group therapists share an emphasis on the therapist's acceptance of the child, first named "social hunger" by Slavson (1943). As relationships and identifi-cations also occur among the children, implicit to this book is the assumption that behavioral and attitudinal changes are made out of increased and continued acceptance by the *therapist and group*. Most traditional models do not highlight the equal impor-tance of the group's acceptance.

An effort has been made to bridge the theory-practice gap, to communicate the art of group psychotherapy with children and adolescents. The experiential intertwining of the relation-ships and the dynamic parallel processes of individual and group dynamics have a multidetermined and multivaried im-pact on the group.

PREMISES

Underlying this relationship-oriented conceptual frame-work and model are attitudinal and operational premises relating to both theory and practice. The process of conceptualizing these premises resulted from the six authors' agreement, influenced by their individual and collective backgrounds, training, and experience.

The first of these premises is that normal childhood contains several developmental stages in the lifelong process of individual growth and development. These developmental stages have clearly recognizable goals, tasks, and milestones that must be experienced before moving onto the next stage. Given a proper amount of nurturance and absence of trauma, a child moves through these stages, even if conflictual, and attains the next stage of development. In times of stress, anxiety, and trauma, the child may regress to earlier conflicts and behavior. A child's progress can be ascertained at any point by evaluating the child's behavioral and psychological phenomena and comparing it with established criteria. Individual differences and dynamics due to environmental and genetic factors are evident in the child's movement in, through, and out of each stage.

Preschool-age children are dealing with separation-individuation issues (Mahler, Pine, & Bergman, 1975). In groups we see them as transferring trusting relationships outside of their homes, learning and practicing social roles and functions with peers. Latency-age children are enmeshed in their struggles of establishing and maintaining close friendships, cooperating and sharing, learning the rules and consequences of participation. There is a predilection for group experiences at this age with a frequent preference for nonverbal modes of communicating (Scheidlinger, 1966). Adolescence is the second chance at establishing themselves outside of the home, transferring dependencies onto the group, and forming intimate relationships. It is seen as a second stage of individuation (Blos, 1979).

In line with developmental thinking, we view children as children, not as diminutive adults. Different expectations are held commensurate with the children's development of cognition, judgment, language, symbolism, insight, impulse control, intuition, observing ego, and ego capabilities. Children become very knowledgeable and sophisticated about themselves and significant others around them, in relationship to their feelings and dynamics at their own levels of development. They can be expected to make age-appropriate decisions and to assume responsibilities for implementing and abiding by their own decisions. Therapists must take care not to expect or attempt to force a child to make decisions at an adult level. Children, especially disturbed ones, need support, instruction, and guidance to develop their abilities in the therapeutic growth process as well as to acquire freedom to use them. Children are entitled to be treated with respect, dignity, and consideration for their being, worth, and feelings as persons.

Groupings, intense feelings, and relationships develop naturally and spontaneously among children, even at early ages. As children advance in age, these groups grow sequentially in organization, cohesiveness, and sophistication. Mueller and Bergstrom (1982) found that the equal nature of peer relations have three basic positive personality aspects associated with them: cooperativeness, playfulness, and friendliness (p. 192). "Early peer relations are shown to foster both specific social skills and a general sense of efficacy," a source of competence (pp. 213–214). Grunebaum and Solomon (1982) have advanced a peer-oriented theory of group therapy. They have formulated developmental stages of friendship formation that they feel are autonomous, sequential systems forming a unique form of "pair bonding." They are momentary physicalistic playmates and an egocentric view (toddlerhood); unilateral partners and one-way assistance (preschoolers); bilateral partners and fair-weather cooperation (middle childhood); chumship and consensual exchange (preadolescence); and intimate and mutually shared friendship (adolescence) (Grunebaum & Solomon, 1982, pp. 285–297).

Another premise is that therapy groups are different from these natural groupings but take into account and utilize understanding of these dynamics and relationships. Therapy groups are led by a qualified therapist who utilizes therapeutic techniques grounded in theory. The group of children are led in the process of changing their behavior, personalities, and emotional lives, which enables them to increase their personal satisfactions

and their interactions with significant others. The defined population, therapeutic goals, techniques employed, theoretical underpinnings, and the qualifications required of the therapist differentiate therapy groups from other groups. The terms *group
psychotherapy* and *group therapy* are used interchangeably in this
volume and are utilized with the knowledge of definitions of
group psychotherapy and social group work (Scheidlinger,
1953; Slavson, 1974).

Group therapy is the treatment of choice for some children
following an evaluation. It is not a panacea for every emotional
disturbance affecting children nor a method to be used simply
because all others have failed.

Children's therapy groups are different from adult therapy
groups, a view firmly held by most children's group therapists.
Developmental differences in cognition, motility, reality testing,
ego organization, identifications, and impulse control cause children to be more active in all stages of group treatment. They act
out openly both in ego mastery and in testing the limits of relationships, utilizing modes of expressing their intense needs that
are different from those used by adults. As a consequence, they
exhibit different therapeutic needs from those of adults. Also,
therapists working with children's therapy groups differ from
therapists who work with adults in similar settings. This is in
great part a result of the differences in the expression of the
needs of children in therapy and in the required responses to
those needs.

A group process approach to children's groups is taken by
the authors. In this book, the terms *group process* and *group dynamics* are used interchangeably. Groups have a group atmosphere, moods, likes and dislikes, that change and vary with activities or discussion. Groups differ in their tolerance of difference
and deviance among members. Groups have levels of manage-
ability. At times they are resistant, disorganized, and fragmented, with breakdowns in controls; whereas at other times
they are cooperative, geared toward ego mastery, and independent in carrying out activities and discussion. Groups can be var-
iously attributed with having a group ego and superego and as
being transitional objects (Levin, 1982) and "mother-group"
(Scheidlinger, 1974). ·

Every children's treatment group is viewed as having a similar developing process. This process differs only in sophistication of its form, the level of awareness in the children and therapist, and mode of expression due to developmental levels, age, and pathology of the group. It begins before the beginning of the group and continues beyond the group's end. The group dynamics can be used as a vehicle of change when influenced by the therapist and the group. Individual dynamics and behavior also are recognized and observed for both relevance to the individual and impact on the group. The therapist observes, formulates, and handles these multiple levels of relationships. In children's groups, these relationships extend beyond the group itself and extend themselves to parents, consultants, teachers, and agencies. The process evolves in a parallel fashion at many different levels, each affecting the other in varying ways and degrees.

A group process approach encompasses the conceptual gestalt that therapy groups are more than the sum total of all their parts. This premise holds that groups are an entity to which group members relate and of which they are a part. The fields of group dynamics and group psychotherapy have developed largely in isolation from one another. Their potential contributions to one another were the subject of the 1957 and October 1963 issues of the *International Journal of Group Psychotherapy*, a book by Durkin (1964), and an article by Lieberman, Lakin, and Whitaker (1969).

Slavson gave recognition to group processes in 1946, indicating that group therapy had been evaluated only in terms of its effects on the individual and that there was a need for greater understanding of what occurred within the group to produce the therapeutic effect, the intragroup process. He wrote, "Group therapy as a tool in treatment will come into its own when the group dynamics are understood" (Slavson, 1946, p. 669). Later Slavson (1957) carefully distinguished between group dynamics and interpersonal interactions. He defined the common purpose of the group as patients having the same purpose of achieving individual relief of suffering and personality deficiencies, rather than there being a common group aim. He argued that although group dynamics are present, they are not permitted to operate and are "nipped in the bud" (Slavson, 1957, p. 145). Slavson concluded that the process of individuation prevented the development of group cohesion.

In 1954 Scheidlinger observed that group psychotherapy follows the dynamics of treatment and that most group theoretical writings concentrated on individual behavioral patterns and phases of therapeutic process. "Group psychological aspects which in all probability are basically the same for all face-to-face groups have been largely neglected" (Scheidlinger, 1954, p. 143). Attention that has been paid to them, he adds, has largely been as they tend to interfere, such as resistance, scapegoating, conflict between cliques, and reactions to new members.

In 1957, Anthony (Foulkes & Anthony, 1973) defined psychodynamics as including both individual and group dynamics. He discusses where to place the focus, whether on the individual, the group as a whole, or the interactions between the members (pp. 141–144). The group analyst's focus is not fixated but flexible, constantly shifting from intraindividual to interindividual depending on the events and circumstances. This flexibility and need to empathize with the group as a whole and with each individual member creates heavy demands. The therapist's attention is oscillatory, the focus being determined by the vicissitudes of the therapy and his or her professional experience. Experience develops this capacity for multiple attention. Anthony's analogy is to a spectator's ability to follow individual plays, team, and partner interaction, and eventually to umpire decisions in team tennis. "It would, in fact, be difficult to maintain dichotomized interest since both individual and group are vividly present all the time" (Foulkes & Anthony, 1973, p. 143). A further contribution to group psychotherapy dynamics theory is Anthony's group phenomenology, including socialization, "mirror" phenomena, "condenser" phenomena, "chain" phenomena, resonance, and group ego. He concludes that "there is no group therapy without group dynamics, and group dynamics is essential to the understanding of group therapy" (Foulkes & Anthony, 1973, p. 182).

Day (1981) adds his perspective that "some of the apparent controversy over individual versus group dynamics . . . may be an expression of styles congenial to particular therapists and not a matter of dogma" (p. 156–157). He views individual and group dynamics as "intermeshed in making group therapy effective for its members" (p. 155).

Group psychotherapy books integrating group process conceptualization have been on the increase, thus creating more interest. This began in 1954 with Bach, followed in 1957 by Foulkes and Anthony, Whitaker and Lieberman in 1964, Yalom in 1970, and Levine in 1979. There has not been a book published on children's group therapy focusing on and integrating group process conceptualization with group psychotherapy. Redl and Wineman (1957) come close but cover broader areas than group psychotherapy. Speers and Lansing's (1965) group process orientation is limited because of their population of preschool psychotics. Rose (1972) has integrated group dynamics with behavior modification.

The manner in which the group process progresses from the beginning to the ending of the group is conceptualized in developmental stages by the authors. This premise views every children's therapy group as having a similar, ongoing, developing group process with recognizable stages, each with goals, tasks, and milestones that are observable and understandable and that can be utilized to accomplish individual and group treatment goals. These accomplishments need completion before moving on to the next stage. Passage through the stages is influenced by the therapist's actions, the children's dynamics, and the group's balance and dynamics. The group is vulnerable to stress, trauma, and lack of nurturance, much like the individual progressing through life's developmental stages. Because of these factors, not all groups pass through all of the stages. Their movement through the stages varies in ease, fluidity, and speed. Some regress, some fixate, and some have peaks and valleys, whereas others move in a fairly steady progression. Therapeutic benefits do occur simply with the passage through each stage.

Within the group-development literature, the theoretical issue arises whether these stages are really as evident or as stratified as some propose or whether progression is more linear or cyclical. Whitaker and Lieberman (1964) indicate a cyclical process of issues, dealt with at a different and deeper level the next time around. Bach (1954) utilizes a "wave" concept and proposes an elaborate system of themes, communications, resistances, and therapeutic functions. Feldman and Wodarski (1975) assent that the progressive phase concept is practical due to one or a cluster of attributes predominating in one phase as compared with others (p. 49). Yalom (1975) prefers speaking of developmental tasks, as groups rarely permanently graduate from one phase. He sees the phases as having dim boundaries, overlapping, and not being well demarcated but feels a developmental sequence concept is necessary so the therapist can maintain "objectivity and to appreciate the course the group pursues despite considerable yawing" (Yalom, 1975, p. 316).

THEORETICAL COMPONENTS

The following developmental conceptual framework and practice model has been utilized with preschoolers, latency-aged, and adolescents with varying degrees and types of disturbance. It is an attempt to present a view narrow enough to be considered a therapeutic model within a conceptual framework broad enough to encompass the use of existing models of group therapy. Its basic components also may be applied to existing group therapy frameworks and models. It can be practiced in any clinical setting as long as chosen composition, goals, and techniques are consistent and its therapists are qualified. Guidelines allow for variance based upon age, disturbance, setting, and theoretical orientations.

In addition to premises underlying our model, there are several essential theoretical components necessary to explain and encompass its breadth, depth, and flexibility. These components, arising out of an eclectic theoretical and practice background, basically represent a melding and integration of several individual and group psychotherapeutic methods and models. Because of the nature of this framework and the way it evolved, it is difficult to trace and give adequate credit to all of our forebears. In retrospect, we have chosen to identify the basic influences in the literature by way of illustration, agreement, comparison, and contrast.

There are six basic components to the authors' framework and model. It includes a developmental, psychodynamic orientation, incorporating multiple levels of influence and communication. It is a group process approach that has a dual focus on individual dynamics and group dynamics. Here-and-now and then-and-there interpretations of behavior are utilized. A multidimensional focus on the following group relationships are present; therapist and child, child and child, therapist and group, child and group, therapist and therapist. Transference, countertransference, and real-person aspects of these relationships are experientially utilized as indicated. The additional influence of outside relationships with families, school, and agency show themselves within the group.

Group dynamics or process theory is not viewed by the authors as conflictual with individual dynamics. Although aware of this controversy, we view them as separate but parallel developmental lines. The relevance and importance of individual dynamics—the necessity of utilizing, understanding, and interpreting them—is not underestimated, overlooked, nor exclusively focused on. The therapist utilizes psychodynamic information to help individuals recognize, understand, and influence their own dynamics and to educate the group to its importance and relevance to behavior. Individual and group goals are formulated. Individual and group explanations and interpretations are made when individual behavior speaks for the group, when it becomes central to the group's conflicts, and when it stimulates imitation, produces an echo effect, or is highly contagious. Individual role behavior at times becomes group role behavior and is recognized and utilized therapeutically with a focus on how one influences the other. Subgroups form and often dissolve as quickly as they form. Leadership takes varying forms and formats. Sometimes pairings, cliques, clusters, and collusions form more permanently. There is a natural, easy interchange and flow between individual and group behaviors, which is not contradictory nor combative but is reflective of the dynamics and nature of each particular group and its membership. Each member and the therapist influence or affect every other person and the group by his or her action or lack of it, by successes, failures, crises, comings, and goings. These processes are more apparent during the *cohesive stage* when parallel associations and transferences are explored (Day, 1981, p. 169).

The therapist structures interpretations in the simplest form, focusing first on the here-and-now, observed defenses and behavior seen in the group. He or she is always mindful of the timing and simplicity. Schiffer (1977) utilizes the term *explanation* as being more accurate than *interpretation* because of the children's limited thought and ideational capacities (p. 383). Understanding the nature, purpose, and intent of these helps the child, therapist, and group to feel more comfortable and safe and to learn alternative modes of coping. With time and further understanding, this may include identifying how this environment is not a repetition of his or her past, as may have been expected and anticipated. Often simply experiencing strong emotional expression in an accepting group environment is sufficient. For children, resonance to earlier experiences is not always in the distant past, as they daily experience poor relationships with parents, siblings, and peers. More often the therapist works toward derivative insight, acquired nonverbally over a period of time through experience, rather than the more complex, psychological insight. This derivative insight is the child's capacity to sense changes in his behavior and within himself as a result of therapy; "the child reflectively begins to see himself in a new light" (Schiffer, 1977, p. 382). This insight is "often a result rather than a cause of improvement" (Ginott, 1975, p. 355). Because of the "uncrystallized" nature of the children's personalities and character, "new, corrective experiences in psychotherapy can be internalized" (Schiffer, 1977, p. 382).

This framework has a multidimensional focus on group relationships as acceptance and closeness are sought and feared and accompanied by anxiety. Object relations theory has been utilized by Kosseff (1975) to develop the concept of how the group serves the function of a transitional object. This theoretical advance demonstrates how the group serves both intrapsychic and interpersonal functions at the same time. The group serves as a bridge for children trying to emancipate themselves from a symbiotic tie to the therapist. It allows for a healthy identification process with the group (pp. 233–235).

Due to the age, cognitive ability, and time proximity of children to their normal developmental and pathological crises and conflicts, transference reactions are not always clearly crystallized, developed, and evident. Emotions may not be repressed, and the therapist and/or children do not become a replacement object. An expectation and emotional reaction is strong and apparent but not always clearly transferential. Grotjahn (1972) views group therapy as the treatment of choice for adolescents, as the "family neurosis" is transferred to the group enabling it to be reenacted, reexperienced, interpreted, and worked through (p. 173).

Therapist countertransference is especially strong and evident in work with children and adolescents. Evans (1965) indicates the acknowledgment and use of it as a therapeutic tool is a recent development. Children's and adolescents' projective defenses, ambivalence, and limited internal controls are normal, innate, and intense. They easily become dependent on an idealized parental figure. The therapist can just as easily fall into wanting to rescue, protect, and nurture. Evans views projective defenses as enabling the adolescent to become disappointed and detached, allowing him or her to become independent (p. 269). Grotjahn (1972) recommends the use of co-therapists to stimulate further the family transference and to help evaluate the therapist's countertransferences.

Partly because of the strength of the projective defenses, it is often a long, slow process for the child or adolescent and the group to recognize and appreciate the real-person aspects of the therapist. Often not until the therapist is pushed to reveal his or her real feelings of anger and hurt during stages III and IV are the child and group finally able to trust the therapist's empathy, understanding, and caring. The therapist's acknowledgment and sharing of these real-person aspects varies with child and group but help lead to an internalization of the therapist as a real person.

Not only are the intragroup and intergroup relationships influential but so are the outside relationships. Parents are dynamically intertwined. Agency policy, support, and reaction are present and felt both by the therapist and the group. Schools likewise can exhibit influence on the children and therapist, as can colleagues. These relationships are evident in the group in a parallel fashion. There is no literature found outlining and discussing these parallel processes so inherent, especially, in children's groups. Only Soo (1977) has an article correlating a process between the child and parents in group treatment, and Rosenthal (1958) has one on the therapist-group-supervisor triad.

The theoretical approach and the therapeutic model developed from our experiences seems to be explained naturally by dividing the group process into six stages. The beginning stage, *preparation*, takes the therapist from the time of initial commitment to doing a group to the point at which the group is to begin, including the initial contacts with the group candidates and their parents. It deals with the trials and tribulations of starting a group and beginning to form a relationship between the therapist and the individual children. *Exploration* begins with the first session and continues until the group has a labeled identity. *Anxiety*, a most difficult action stage, ends when the children commit themselves to the group process. Intense psychological closeness is present during the *cohesion stage*. *Termination* follows with the recognition of the coming end of the group and finishes when the door closes on the final session. *Closure*, the final stage, takes the therapist from the final session through implementation of the recommendations for future care of the children to final resolution of his or her feelings for the children and the group. Each stage is further delineated by the conceptualization of subphases.

Each stage chapter is organized into three sections. The first, Experiential Description, is an attempt to capture the essence of what is observable in group process from an invisible observer's perspective. The clinical material is reported in this manner in order to provide a fuller picture than would one group's process recording. The clinical examples exemplify a closed, older latency-age group, with exceptions in process noted for younger and older children. Dynamic Description is an explanation and integration of the observable and experiential with the dynamic and the theoretical. It is in this section that the child, therapist, group, parent, and agency are highlighted. Discussion and exploration of clinical techniques and issues arising in each stage requiring special attention are elaborated in the Special Issues section of each chapter.

Therapist Role, Function, and Training

Theoretical, technical, and practical considerations of a group therapy framework or model would be incomplete without a discussion of the therapist's role, responsibility, training, and supervision. The three major mental health professions—psychiatry, psychology, and social work—provide some of the training necessary to conduct therapy groups with children and adolescents. The same training, ethical, clinical, and professional standards adhered to for individual therapists within these professions are assumed to apply also to group therapists. The authors assume that no therapist following these standards would undertake group psychotherapy without some prior training, course work, or supervision. In addition, a competent children's group therapist needs skill in both individual and group psychotherapy.

Yalom (1975) and Levine (1979) outline training criteria for group therapists. Yalom includes four experiences: to observe experienced group therapists at work, to have clinical supervision of his or her early groups, to have a personal group experience, and to have personal psychotherapeutic or self-exploratory work (p. 504). Ginott (1961) also stresses that to work with children a theoretical knowledge of psychosexual development is necessary, as is supervised experience in individual and group play therapy, activity, and interview therapy. "Experience alone cannot be a substitute for supervised training; ten years of work may in reality add up to no more than one year of error-full experience and nine years of repetition" (Ginott, 1961, p. 125).

Any therapist involved with children needs certain qualities, above and beyond the professional qualifications, as the therapist's personality is of utmost importance in the success of treatment. Among these are the following: that he or she see children as special people needing and responding to respect and courtesy; that he or she genuinely like children; that he or she can bridge the years and psychological gaps to be truly empathetic with children. We agree with Ginott's statement that the therapist must like children but must not have a strong need to be liked by them (p. 127). He cautions that "every therapist should have a clear appreciation of the particular gratifications that he derives from working with children" (Ginett, 1961, p. 133). An ability to communicate verbally and nonverbally with children on an effective level and a high degree of frustration tolerance and resilience are important. It helps to retain that special wonder of childhood that triggers enthusiasm, spontaneity, curiosity, and exploration, as does an appreciation of the joys that only children can bring. Additionally, we assume that the therapist can give and receive affection, play comfortably, and get dirty, and that he or she has both patience with and tolerance for children's expression through activity. The therapist must be young enough in spirit or years to still have "those irrational qualities of youth that enable grownups to stand, withstand, and understand children" (Ginott, 1961, p. 127). These qualities apply equally to adolescent-group therapists with variance according to the differing tasks of adolescence. Some therapists are able to work equally effectively with both age groups, whereas others cannot.

The role of the group therapist with children and adolescents is seen as being an active, involved, responsive one, sensitized to the psychosocial needs of the developmental age of the group and to the manifestation of disturbance. At all times, support and facilitation are uppermost in the therapist's mind and action, even when utilizing the techniques of confrontation, interpretation, clarification, and intervention. The main role of the therapist is to create a consistently predictable atmosphere that motivates learning about oneself and others. This necessitates providing enough security, acceptance, limits, and respect, which varies with the child and the group, to allow expression and exploration of their innermost selves and strivings. As the children experience the therapist's consistent, nonjudgmental attitude, they are freed to reveal and face their feelings more openly. As they experience the inherent importance of boundaries and limits, free of the therapist's guilt and anxiety, they are freed to individuate and develop self-identity. As they feel accepted, respected, and appreciated, they are able to feel a sense of self-worth. Only through this all-accepting, consistently caring relationship, first with the therapist and through him with the group, will the children be able to counteract the inconsistent, sometimes threatening manner in which they were treated in the past. These real aspects of the therapist, his reaction and response to the child and his behavior, are of prime consideration to the child.

The role of the therapist is partially defined by its primary emphasis on the use of therapeutic communication focusing on relationships. The developing relationship follows the course of any therapeutic relationship except that it is done in a group. The therapist must be active in an open, honest, and direct manner, consistently communicating and establishing this through word and action. This includes an understanding of the parameters and limits of the room, equipment, and relationships. Acceptance of thoughts and feelings and their confidentiality are issues needing explanation and repeated assurance.

The manner in which the therapist accepts and deals with anxiety, anger, aggression, testing, acting-out, resistance, conflicts, leadership, rules, and decision-making also conveys this therapeutic role and stance. How the therapist is able to demonstrate, simultaneously and consecutively, his or her concern, caring, and developing relationship with each child, the group, and a co-therapist reinforces this emphasis on the relationships within the group.

In order to accomplish this consistent approach, the therapist must have theoretical understanding and rationale to increase both the ease of decision-making and his or her confidence. As the therapist sees the structure and arena in which these complex therapeutic relationships and communications take place, he or she needs the support of his or her convictions. The more information and knowledge the therapist has of individual psychodynamics, group dynamics, developmental theory, object relations theory, ego psychology, peer relations theory, and behavioral theory, the more complete will be this understanding and rationale. All is not apparent as it meets the eye; it also must meet the mind and connect with the body affect. The therapist must also stay in touch with his or her intuition, integrating mind and body theory.

What is seen and heard in the group of the therapist's own feelings and reactions relates to the therapist's awareness, comfort, and theoretical support for their exposure. The therapist need not reveal all he or she is aware of, nor hold back when he or she judges it appropriate and necessary to share. The stage of the group, the core issues being dealt with, and the pathology of the children, signal the timing, nature, and degree of disclosure.

In their work on peer-oriented theory of group therapy, Grunebaum and Solomon (1980) advise the therapist to be a participant-facilitator, responsive, open, accepting, and confident, and most of all he or she should foster better peer relationships and group formation (p. 42). Anthony states that there is a "constant centripetal centrifugal movement of the group as a whole in relation to the therapist" (Foulkes & Anthony, 1973, p. 210). Slavson (1943) views the therapist's role in activity group therapy as an "ideal parent," giving unconditional acceptance. Sugar (1974) views it not as being a better, gratifying parent but as an interpreter and encourager of participation with other children. Battegay (1975) sees the leader's role as being attentive to the group process and individuals while at the same time remaining in the background as a moderator and facilitator. Helping the members find ways to contribute, involves them in the three important factors of analytic work, repeating, insight, and social learning (p. 101).

Co-therapy

Whether or not to utilize a co-therapist with children's and adolescents' treatment groups is often a decision relating to agency structure and expectations and/or therapists' theoretical expectations and orientation. Theoretical, economic, and training issues are sometimes more involved in the choice than therapeutic considerations.

The use and effectiveness of co-therapists is a relatively unexplored and unresearched area. Although its use was often begun for training purposes, it was soon discovered that certain transferences and dynamics occurred spontaneously due to the presence of two therapists. This has opened up a new territory of information. More has been written in relationship to advantages and disadvantages of utilizing co-therapists with adult groups (Levine, 1979; Lundin & Aronov, 1969; Yalom, 1970, 1975). Two therapists simulate a family environment and offer two observations, perspectives, and expertise. Co-therapy allows easy stimulation of transferences, a splitting of ambivalence between the two, and utilization of splitting techniques such as support and confrontation. Two carefully chosen therapists can complement each other's strengths and weaknesses. Their relationship can serve as a successful role model for relationships for the children and provide professional and personal growth and learning for the therapists.

An advantage, especially unique and important with some children's groups, is a reduction of anxiety surrounding controls. Limit setting can be easier with an acting-out group; one therapist deals with the group while the other deals with the acting-out member. Due to their feelings of helplessness and impotence, those members exhibiting conflicts with authority often try to undermine, intrude, and split the two therapists. Use of co-therapists can allow for the therapeutic splitting of the control function, which is especially helpful with adolescents: One therapist can become "one of the group" while the other can remain in control (Grotjahn, 1972).

One disadvantage inherent in co-therapy is the considerable time and effort required to communicate about the individual members, the group, and the co-therapy relationship. An independent practitioner may feel uncomfortable with the necessity of sharing decisions, techniques, control, and personal reactions with another therapist, as he or she may feel exposed and vulnerable. A tremendous drawback occurs if the co-therapists are unable to develop a good relationship. A poor co-therapy relationship may evolve into the group's acting-out the therapists' difficulties and may not provide adequate modeling of relationships (Levine, 1979). Yalom (1975) states the importance of equal status, competence, and sensitivity, so as to decrease tension and lack of clarity, and advises establishing only a co-equal status between co-therapists.

Heilfron (1969) focuses on what she feels is the essence of co-therapy, the relationship between the therapists, as an influential factor in the outcome of the treatment. When they like and respect each other, trust, and establish a bond, they can possibly engage in a discovery of their own interrelationship. A progression develops, from separate individuals working together to a sense of we-ness in partnership, which requires deep personal investment and commitment.

Lundin and Aronov (1969) expand on the simulated family experience with its unique learning and broader dynamic areas. Patients naturally respond to one therapist with a major primary reaction of dependency, anger, seduction, or ambivalence. This therapist is seen as more aggressive or masculine, whereas the other therapist is seen as assuming protective, feminine qualities. One therapist tends to be feared, the other idealized (p. 198).

Gallogly and Levine (Levine, 1979) clearly elucidate the unique, differentiated role techniques available for use with co-therapists after they have achieved a degree of mutuality. One co-therapist can help a patient connect or respond to the other co-therapist, complete or reinterpret an intervention begun by the other. Support and confrontation can be split between the two to help deal with resistance and rigidity in the group. Ambivalence sometimes can be resolved by each co-therapist supporting one side of it. Gallogly and Levine identify five developmental phases of the co-therapy relationship that parallel the therapy group's crises and developmental stages (pp. 299–304). Yalom (1970) feels that with co-therapists anger and attack from a group member on one of the therapists can easily be explored as an issue by the other. The existence of the other also helps to maintain objectivity in the face of "massive group pressure" (p. 320).

There are several exceptions to a co-equal status between the co-therapists. When utilized for training purposes, an unequal status may be accepted, but it has its own complex, inherent conflicts, dynamics, and issues. Sometimes co-therapy roles are split into practitioner and observer. In his work with delinquent boys, Kassoff (1958) felt that the co-therapy interrelationship was important and effective with a neophyte and an experienced therapist. Gallogly and Levine (Levine, 1979) caution that a trainee should have more than just the one co-therapy relationship with his trainer in order not to have a one-sided view. It may also be important to experience sole leadership or another co-therapy relationship concurrently. The authors advise all novice and experienced therapists to have more than one group running concurrently, in order to maintain a perspective on one's competence when groups run into difficulties, and to appreciate the uniqueness yet commonness of each group.

CONSULTATION AND SUPERVISION

The necessity of supervision and consultation is supported by Kadis, Krasner, Winick, and Foulkes (1963) as they caution against some "wild cat" therapists conveying "the idea that supervision is not necessary" (p. 34). In areas where adequate supervision is unavailable locally they suggest hiring competent people to come in weekly or semimonthly from another area. To neglect supervision "in the practice of group psychotherapy is as dangerous as it would be in any other therapeutic endeavor" (Kadis et al. p. 34). "A supervised clinical experience is a *sine qua non* in the education of the group therapist" and in many ways is "more taxing than individual therapy supervision" (Yalom, 1975, p. 506). "Mastering the cast of characters is, in itself, a formidable task," in addition to the necessity of a "highly selective focus" on the "abundance of data" (p. 506).

It seems superfluous to note that the therapist should trust and respect the consultant's judgment. The beginning relationship covers an understanding of the type of therapy planned, the nature of the children's disturbances, what and how much advice the therapist wishes, the techniques the consultant uses, and how much, if any, responsibility he or she will be asked to or is willing to assume for the therapy.

As therapy progresses, the consultant tries to maintain an objective view of what is happening to the children and the therapist, what themes are evident, and what the interactive effect is of the following relationships: therapist and child, therapist and group, co-therapists, therapist and consultant, and consultant to group through the therapist. There are also the relationships of child and parent, therapist and parent, consultant and parent through the therapist, and all of the above with the agency. The therapist may need help in relieving his or her own anxieties, fears, and doubts in order to develop emotional insulation against anxieties induced by the group (Rosenthal, 1968). It is the consultant's role and responsibility to convey his or her observations and assessments of what is happening within the group including the effect of the therapist's role and actions to the therapist in the least critical way possible in order to be of assistance. Decision-making rests with the therapist, as does determination of how he or she may make the best use of the information.

The supervisor's role, although similar to the consultant's, has a few distinct differences. In general, the supervisor retains a great deal more responsibility for the therapy than does a consultant. He or she is usually also responsible for the training and professional growth of the trainee. Consequently, the supervisor will not only assess the data, giving his or her opinion to the therapist, but will define, label, and illustrate the processes as they occur, while describing and recommending techniques. This role should find a balance between supporting, leading, and guiding, yet promote enough independence in the trainee. Throughout the process, the supervisor should never lose sight of the fact that his or her first responsibility must be to safeguard the well-being of the children while guiding trainees in increasing their therapeutic skills. Appreciating these differences, in this volume the terms supervision and consultation are mostly used generically and interchangeably.

Joint supervision of co-therapists, also called triadic supervision, should be held, with a triadic focus on the development of the co-therapy relationship and its effects on the group, as well as the assessment of the group and its members. It is both appropriate and helpful to work on some aspects of the co-therapists' egalitarian relationship. Supervision can have a stabilizing influence on both co-therapists over a period of time and can examine the effect of the co-therapy relationship on the group (McGee, 1974). Gallogly and Levine (Levine, 1979) recommend that co-therapists meet both alone and with a supervisor, bringing to supervision those issues they are not able to work out together.

The format for group consultation can follow a more traditional individual method of supervision, can be held in a group, or can have a group workshop format. Such sessions can focus on ongoing groups, group processes, and specific problems. Use of process transcripts, tape recordings, one-way screen observations, and videotaping all have been found valuable.

If supervision of groups is impossible to obtain, Kadis et al. (1963) suggest regular meetings of those involved in group therapy, focusing on continuous case presentation and/or discussion of special problems. These meetings may offer educational help as well as resolution of difficulties. They observe that objective listeners "may help to pick up and clarify disruptive influences like countertransference factors operating in the group" (Kadis et al., 1963, p. 34). Our observation is that it helps to have experienced clinicians present who are used to observing transference and countertransference phenomena, even if in individual settings, rather than just a peer group of novice therapists.

REFERENCES

Bach, G. S. (1954). *Intensive group psychotherapy*. New York: Ronald Press.

Battegay, R. (1975). The leader and group structure. In Z. A. Liff (Ed.), *The leader in the group*. New York: Jason Aronson. pp. 95–103.

Blos, P. (1979). *The adolescent passage*. New York: International Universities Press.

Day, M. (1981). Process in classical psychodynamic groups. *International Journal of Group Psychotherapy, 31*, 153–174.

Durkin, H. E. (1964). *The group in depth*. New York: International Universities Press.

Evans, J. (1965). In-patient analytic group therapy of neurotic and delinquent adolescents; some specific problems associated with these groups. *Psychotherapy and Psychosomatics, 13*, 265–270.

Feldman, R. A., & Wodarski, J. S. (1975). *Contemporary approaches to group treatment*. San Francisco: Jossey-Bass.

Foulkes, S. H., & Anthony, E. J. (1973). *Group psychotherapy: The psychoanalytic approach* (rev. 2nd ed.). Baltimore: Penguin Books.

Ginott, H. G. (1961). *Group psychotherapy with children*. New York: McGraw-Hill.

Ginott, H. G. (1975). Group therapy with children. In G. M. Gazda

(Ed.), *Basic approaches to group psychotherapy and group counseling* (2nd ed.). Springfield, IL: Charles C Thomas. pp. 272–294.

Grotjahn, M. (1972). The therapeutic dynamics of the therapeutic group experience. In I. H. Berkovitz (Ed.). *Adolescents grow in groups*. New York: Brunner/Mazel. pp. 173–178.

Grunebaum, H., & & Solomon, L. (1980). Toward a peer theory of group psychotherapy: 1. On the developmental significance of peers and play. *International Journal of Group Psychotherapy, 30*, 23–49.

Grunebaum, H., & Solomon, L. (1982). Toward a theory of peer relationships: 2. On the stages of social development and their relationship to group psychotherapy. *International Journal of Group Psychotherapy, 32*, 283–307.

Heilfron, M. (1969). Co-therapy: The relationship between therapists. *International Journal of Group Psychotherapy, 19*, 366–381.

Kadis, A. L., Krasner, J. D., Winick, C., & Foulkes, S. H. (1963). *A practicum of group psychotherapy*. New York: Harper & Row.

Kassoff, A. I. (1958). Advantages of multiple therapists in a group of severely acting-out adolescent boys. *International Journal of Group Psychotherapy, 8*, 70–75.

Kosseff, J. W. (1975). The leader using object-relations theory. In Z. A. Liff (Ed.), *The leader in the group*. New York: Jason Aronson. pp. 212–242.

Levin, S. (1982). The adolescent group as transitional object. *International Journal of Group Psychotherapy, 32*, 217–232.

Levine, B. (1979). *Group psychotherapy practice and development*. Englewood Cliffs, NJ: Prentice-Hall.

Lieberman, M. A., Lakin, M., & Whitaker, D. S. (1969). Problems and potential of psychoanalytic and group-dynamic theories for group psychotherapy. *International Journal of Group Psychotherapy, 19*, 131–141.

Lundin, W. H., & Aronov, B. M. (1969). The use of co-therapists in group psychotherapy. In H. M. Ruitenbeck (Ed.), *Group therapy today*. New York: Atherton Press. pp. 195–202.

Mahler, M. S., Pine, F., & Bergman, A. (1975). *The psychological birth of the human infant*. New York: Basic Books.

McGee, T. F. (1974). The triadic approach to supervision in group psychotherapy. *International Journal of Group Psychotherapy, 24*, 471–475.

Mueller, E., & Bergstrom, J. (1982). Fostering peer relations in young normal and handicapped children. In K. M. Borman (Ed.), *The social life of children in a changing society* Hillsdale, NJ: Lawrence Erlbaum. pp. 191–215.

Redl, F., & Wineman, D. (1957). *The aggressive child.* New York: Free Press.

Rose, S. D. (1972). *Treating children in groups: A behavioral approach.* San Francisco: Jossey-Bass.

Rosenthal, L. (1958). Some aspects of a triple relation. In A. Esman (Ed.), *New frontiers in child guidance.* New York: International Universities Press. pp. 78–89.

Scheidlinger, S. (1953). The concepts of social group work and group psychotherapy. *Social Casework, 34,* 292–297.

Scheidlinger, S. (1954). Group psychotherapy. *American Journal of Orthopsychiatry, 24,* 140–145.

Scheidlinger, S. (1966). The concept of latency: Implications for group treatment. *Social Casework, 47,* 363–367.

Scheidlinger, S. (1974). On the concept of the "mother-group." *International Journal of Group Psychotherapy, 24,* 417–428.

Schiffer, M. (1977). Activity-interview group psychotherapy: Theory, principles, and practice. *International Journal of Group Psychotherapy, 27,* 377–388.

Slavson, S. R. (1943). *An introduction to group therapy.* New York: International Universities Press.

Slavson, S. R. (1946). Group psychotherapy. In E. Spiegel (Ed.), *Progress in neurology and psychiatry.* New York: Grune & Stratton. pp. 662–680.

Slavson, S. R. (1957). Are there "group dynamics" in therapy groups? *International Journal of Group Psychotherapy, 7,* 131–154.

Slavson, S. R. (1974). Types of group psychotherapy and their clinical applications. In S. DeSchill (Ed.), *The challenge for group psychotherapy.* New York: International Universities Press. pp. 49–119.

Soo, E. S. (1977). The impact of collaborative treatment on premature termination in activity group therapy. *Group, 1,* 222–234.

Speers, R. W., & Lansing, C. (1965). *Group therapy in childhood psychoses.* Chapel Hill, NC: University of North Carolina Press.

Sugar, M. (1974). Interpretive group psychotherapy with latency children. *Journal of the American Academy of Child Psychiatry, 13,* 648–666.

Whitaker, D. S., & Lieberman, M. A. (1964). *Psychotherapy through group process.* New York: Atherton.

Yalom, I. D. (1970). *The theory and practice of group psychotherapy.* New York: Basic Books.

Yalom, I. D. (1975). *The theory and practice of group psychotherapy* (rev. ed.). New York: Basic Books.

Chapter 2

CHILDREN'S AND ADOLESCENTS' GROUP THERAPY LITERATURE

Barbara B. Siepker

The paucity of literature available in the field of children's and adolescents' group therapy is readily observed. The books published in the past 25 years on children's groups can be counted on one hand and are reflective of very different approaches: Ganter, Yeakel, and Polansky (1967), Ginott (1961), Rose (1972), Schiffer (1969), and Slavson and Schiffer (1975). Those on adolescents represent similar numbers: Berkovitz (1972), Brandes and Gardner (1973), MacLennan and Felsenfeld (1968), Rachman (1975), and Sugar (1975). Annual reviews of the group therapy literature have made recurrent observations on the paucity of this literature (Lubin & Lubin, 1973; Lubin, Lubin, & Sargent, 1972; MacLennan & Levy 1967, 1968, 1969, 1970, 1971). In 1979 these reviews combined both categories into one paragraph.

As recently as 1970, MacLennan and Levy observed some questioning of the usefulness of treatment groups. There has also been a lack of quality literature, especially regarding theoretical and technical aspects of group treatment. Rosenbaum and Kraft in 1975 similarly conclude there is "a paucity of clear thinking concerning therapy with children" (p. 60⊦).

PSYCHOANALYTIC MODELS

Psychoanalytic models have been the prime theoretical orientation of the group therapy models for children and adolescents. The various models differ in a matter of degree or emphasis regarding the following theoretical issues: the treatment of the individual in the group versus through the group-as-a-whole; verbalization and interpretation versus experiential learning; the activity level of the therapist regarding permissiveness and limit setting. These differences most often relate to theoretical orientation, population served, and setting.

Historical surveys of the development of group therapy with children and adolescents clearly attribute Slavson with its founding in the 1930s. Appley and Winder (1973) summarize Slavson's impact as allowing activity to replace verbalization of conflicts. Slavson's activity group therapy (1943) for latency-age children is an experiential model for children with modifiable habit, character, and behavior disorders. Strict adherence to the model is required in group composition and therapist's activity. The therapist provides an accepting atmosphere of unrestricted and uninterpreted free play and activity. As a neutral, uninvolved, noninterpretive observer, the therapist assumes an "ideal" parental role of unconditional acceptance and permissiveness (although not sanction), thus allowing the child over several years a "corrective experience." This model's effectiveness is attributed to correct selection and grouping to "psychologically" establish and maintain a dynamic equilbrium and balance of instigators, neutralizers, and neuters (Slavson & Schiffer, 1975, p. 111). Once properly composed, it is largely dependent on the "group curative forces," even though the focus remains throughout on the individual dynamics.

A few years after activity group therapy was developed it was recognized that it was not suitable for all young children and preadolescents. Two other models were then developed under Slavson's direction. The first model, play group therapy, is essentially for children four to six years old, involving the interpretation of the meanings and feeling of the play and behavior. "Using *libido-evoking* materials, the patients reveal through play their life problems . . . and the attendant fears, tensions, confusions, anxieties, anger and other emotions" (Slavson & Schiffer, 1975, p. 355). Information is provided and interpretations are focused on the individual child, geared to his or her understanding, and generally kept at a behavioral level.

Ginott, in addition to growing out of the Slavson tradition, was influenced by Axline's (1947) play group therapy for young children, which utilized symbolic and fantasy play, reflection of feelings, and interpretation. Ginott's model (1961) included latency-age children and focused primary attention on the development and ongoing therapeutic relationship with the therapist. An emotionally active therapist's role requires structuring, therapeutic limit setting, and redirecting undesirable acts, in addition to permitting verbal and symbolic expression of feelings. Permission is conveyed to the children to express themselves freely through the medium of play in their own time and way. The theory and practice of limit setting is fully explored and presented.

The second model, activity-interview group therapy (Gabriel, 1939; Schiffer, 1977; Slavson 1945, 1947), was devised because more seriously disturbed children with behavior disorders were inaccessible to the "ego type treatment, either because of over-intense fears and anxieties or because their uncontrolled hyperactivity and aggressions would prevent the therapeutic climate essential for activity group therapy" (Slavson & Schiffer, 1975, p. 297). A much more flexible model than activity group therapy, it allows for verbalization and interpretation of activity. The therapist plays a more central role, structuring "talking" and "working" parts of the meeting. Most frequently, children are also in individual therapy with the group therapist or another therapist.

Modifications of activity group therapy began as early as the 1930s under Slavson's direction. This was followed in the 1940s by Scheidlinger's work with severely damaged and culturally deprived children (1960, 1965). These children, from families with severe social and economic deprivation, experienced neglect, inconsistency, and harsh physical punishment. Serious disturbances in the children's ego developments and functioning resulted, including problems of impulse control, oral fixation, poor reality testing, distortions in perceiving others, poor self-image, and confused identity. Necessary changes in group therapy included active structuring of a consistent, nurturant group climate, frequent therapist activity in direct, emotional reactions, verbal interventions in the form of confronting and clarifying reality, and physical restraint in light of uncontrollable impulsivity.

The 1960s focused on the inadequacies of programs, children's and adolescents' group therapy included, to deal with the numbers of socially disadvantaged urban dwellers. Frank and Zilbach (1968) voiced their concern that activity group therapy had not kept pace due to lack of proper training facilities, the need for a specific physical setting, and greater comfort with talking therapy. They called for continued solid footing within the tradition of activity group therapy with disturbance and setting modifications. MacLennan (1977), sharing this concern, made an even stronger, impassioned plea. In 1969 Schiffer outlined changes in activity group therapy necessary for a therapeutic play group in a school setting with younger children, six to nine years old. The therapist, although substantially permissive and dynamically neutral, is more involved due to the ages of the children, at times intervening for safety. Consistent with activity group therapy, interpretations are not made.

The 1970s brought a resurgence of suggested modifications of activity group therapy, both within and outside of the Slavson tradition, based on population and setting differences and demands. VanScoy (1971) suggested modifications of activity group therapy based on setting and population differences. Seriously disturbed "cast-offs" and "rejects" in a residential treatment setting were treated in small groups of four to five, with co-therapists playing very active roles, structuring activities, limits, and rewards. Epstein and Altman (1972) described their experiences in successfully converting an activity group to verbal group therapy, as a permissive free play atmosphere seemed to work "against ego integration and toward encouragement of random, regressive acting-out behavior" in these boys evidencing power manipulations (p. 95). Similarly, Strunk and Witkin (1974) describe changing a girls' activity group into a discussion group. These girls with deficient inner controls also needed clearly defined limits and expectations, which they came to internalize, actively helping one another to achieve self-control.

Frank (1976) has developed the clearest, most detailed theoretical conceptualization of group therapy with ego-impoverished children since Scheidlinger. Reviewing activity group therapy, she documents the different needs in the setting, structure, and composition of the group and the role of the therapist that is necessitated by these children. In order to meet the therapeutic needs of safety, acceptance, and nurturance, the therapist must provide protective limits (as opposed to punishment) when the children's egos are threatened and in danger of being overwhelmed, and must simultaneously teach the children to expand their ego capacities. The latter approaches include teaching the use of talking as an ego capacity to replace action in these children who have not yet learned this secondary ego function, and the use of the device of role playing to teach ego perception. These children should be grouped together, as they feel safer with others with similar problems. The therapist, therefore, must provide the balance in the missing ego resources within the group.

Due to the far-reaching influence of Slavson's contributions, group therapy with children has virtually been equated with activity group therapy. One unfortunate result of this equation, noted by Sands and Golub in 1974, has been that not only has there been wholesale misapplication to unintended populations and settings but activity per se has become equated with treatment. Charach (1983) observes that therapists have "tried everything to improve on the still influential paradigm of activity group therapy"; those methods combining activity and talking "often begin with an 'apologia' for any method that deviates from activity group therapy" (p. 349). The lack of sorting out the inherent clinical and technical necessities of activity group therapy and the psychoanalytic and child developmental theoretical aspects of the model has added to the confusion in the author's opinion. In addition, activity group therapy has been more frequently highlighted than activity-interview therapy, a model more similar to many models currently practiced in clinics.

Several psychoanalytic group therapy models have developed outside of the Slavson tradition. A relationship therapy model conceived by Dr. John Levy in the 1930s utilized children's and concurrent mothers' groups in a child guidance center (Durkin, 1939, Glatzer & Durkin, 1944, Lowrey, 1944). The therapeutic relationship was considered the essence of the treatment. The therapist's role in a permissive play atmosphere was clearly defined to include the timing of interpretations, stressing the necessity for thorough training, experience, and judgment. This model is not to be confused with the authors', which focuses not only on therapy *in* the group but *through* and *by* the group.

Redl's broad theoretical and practice contributions have centered on translating psychodynamic theory into everyday practice in the fields of child development, education, delinquency, and group therapy. Appley and Winder (1973) attribute Redl with "translating psychoanalytic concepts into the language of group process" (p. 3). From the onset Redl differed with Slavson regarding the issue of therapist activity, questioning on a theoretical and clinical basis the total permissiveness and noninterference of the therapist (Redl & Wineman, 1957). The delinquent population Redl worked with necessitated more active ego interventions to maintain, replace, and strengthen ego functioning under the pressures of group process. Redl and Wineman's model is representative of an integrated psychoanalytic and group-process-oriented model. Redl's theoretical contributions in the area of group process are unparalleled. They include shock effect, group contagion (1949), group composition, group resistances, and group psychological roles (1966). Less well known are the impact of group exposure on ego integrity, the conflicting demands of group membership on the individual personality, exculpation magic through the initiatory act, spatial repetition compulsion, and group intoxifying forces (1942).

Speers and Lansing (1965) described the development of group process in a group of preschool psychotic children and collateral groups of mothers and fathers over a 4-year period. Therapy began with the child needing to maintain his symbiosis supported by massive denial and psychotic fantasy. In the first 3 months of treatment, wild panic reactions resulted from the terrifying closeness of others as the child lost ego boundaries, body image and identity, impulse and affect control. Physical holding to ensure his safety was necessary to help the child endure this phase. These ego functions gradually developed through a process of therapeutic symbiosis with the "group ego" that had developed. Anthony (1973) comments that this slow group development ends where most neurotic groups begin, as the authentic group processes beginning when individuation is present (p. 231). Similar group process was present with autistic and schizophrenic children seen for only a year by Gratton and Rizzo (1969).

Considerably more group process in groups of schizophrenic children is reported by Lifton and Smolen (1966). Their total approach, termed relationship group psychotherapy, appears to be close in nature to the approach of this book. It is based on the theory that childhood schizophrenia results from an original disturbance of relationship, which leads to an inability to establish a relationship to self, objects, and people. All activities are utilized to develop and maintain a relationship with the therapist and children, including therapeutic utilization of resistances, transferences, and countertransferences. Children are treated both as unique individuals and as members of a group. The therapist's role is active and involved; setting clear limits, protecting by verbal and physical restraint, initiating breaking down of autistic barriers, verbalizing and interpreting behavior and feeling at a level that can be understood and assimilated, sensitizing children to each other's problems, feelings, and actions, aligning himself or herself with the child's ego, stopping and interpreting acting-out and self-destructive behavior. It is Lifton and Smolen's belief that group therapy may be the treatment of choice for schizophrenic children, as the group process offers the most effective way to promote socialization. The group forces recognition of other children, provides the constancy, external structure, control, and cohesiveness these children need, and helps them establish increasing affective contact with their surroundings without feeling overwhelmed or threatened.

Anthony (1973) has elaborated three separate group analytic psychotherapy models for children and adolescents in a chapter of a book that unfortunately has gone out of print. These group analytic models, originally developed in England, are both psychoanalytic and group process in conceptualization, with all of the group's communications and relationships being brought back to the group and the therapist for analysis. All members play an active part, although the therapist remains the primary transference figure. The "small table" method, employed with four- to six-year-olds, resembles play therapy with symbolic play content and is held twice weekly. The table setup structures five individual territories and a common territory, with individual sets of play equipment in separate colors. The therapist plays a part, with his own territory and equipment. Concrete and verbal transactions occur, as does group development, which begins with individual play, their parallel play with "collective monologues," and finally "collective fantasies." Anthony's "small room" method for latency-age children is a modification of Slavson's method, taking activity needs into account. Originally a talking period was followed by an activity period, but gradually this became more verbal, analytic, and interpretive, with a focus on the positive and negative aspects of the group. Activity occurred spontaneously, becoming a matter for discussion as it happened. The only explicit rule is "no exit" from the room. For the more acting out group the transformation to verbalizing is difficult to handle and uncomfortable for the therapist but absolutely necessary for their treatment. Adolescents are treated with a "small circle" technique. These groups are characterized by fast-changing, regressive-progressive movement and require a high degree of therapist flexibility.

Interpretive group psychotherapy with outpatient groups has been formulated for latency-age children in an article by Sugar (1974). It is designed for children exhibiting behavioral and neurotic disorders, including psychosomatics, who are able to verbalize. In a relatively ungratifying playroom setting "designed to facilitate the demonstration of conflicts, defenses, and fantasies through verbalization and play" (Sugar, 1974, p. 648), the therapist interprets the child's feelings. Maintaining a friendly, informal role, the therapist encourages the child to participate in play with other children, but does not gratify the child directly or aim to be a "better parent." At times the play may need limiting when it becomes disorganizing or destructive.

Schachter (1974, 1984) has formulated a group therapy model for children who have difficulties verbalizing their feelings and for depressed children. Kinetic psychotherapy utilizes children's games as the medium of interaction, serving as a catalyst for emotions. As emotions are experienced and characteristic responses shown, "a process called 'stop the action' is invoked by the therapist" (1984, p. 85). Identification, verbalization, feedback, and association are encouraged as a part of the discussion.

Blotcky, Sheinbein, Wiggins, and Forgotson (1980) describe a verbal, nondirective, insight-oriented group technique for ego-defective children in an inpatient setting. The therapist's role is permissive and interpreting. Blotcky et al. present a review of latency, emphasizing that older latency-age children possess sufficient abstract and cognitive skills to verbalize present and past experiences. They describe how verbal therapy enhances internal structure and impulse control in these children and how transference reactions and group process can be put to therapeutic use. They describe two group phases: resistance, during which the expression of thoughts, feelings and recreated previous conflictual relationships leads to tumultuous behavior with increasing anxiety and guilt; and the treatment phase, which is cohesive, with the children exhibiting increased internal controls.

The 1980s have brought new theoretical developments. Trafimow and Pattak (1981, 1982) offer a theoretical review of the developmental line of object relations, applying it to group process with very disturbed children exhibiting serious ego deficits, developmental delays, and primitive personality structures. They outline three growth-inducing aspects of group process that are offered within the group: other children as objectal alternatives, group therapists as auxiliary egos, and the group as symbiotic mother. Levin (1982), also utilizing object relations theory, focuses on the adolescent process of individuation. By utilizing the group as a transitional object and an instrument of change, the adolescents shed their infantile dependencies on the therapist through healthy identification processes with peers.

SHORT-TERM MODELS

Short-term models received some attention in the 1960s and 1970s, particularly within clinics and school settings, where the pressure for short-term service is heavy. Therapy groups in the schools vary in goals, structure, and length, from 6 to 12 sessions (Barcai & Robinson, 1969; Gratton & Pope, 1972; Rhodes, 1973).

The length of treatment in outpatient clinics varies from 6 sessions to 6 months. Karson (1965), working with acting-out and neurotic boys, structured concurrent children's and mothers' groups, each run by a therapist and an observer for a period of 6 months. Ganter et al. (1967) focused on an alternative 6-month intensive group treatment experience for children suitable for residential placement. Concrete goals were accomplished through firm, consistent structure and limits. Innovative therapeutic techniques included refusing to become engaged in the struggle, depersonalizing the sources of structure, distracting-decompressing, isolating, insisting on external demands, pacing expectations, avoiding competition, giving freedom within the structure, regrouping, and providing structural change experiences. Pelosi and Friedman (1974) utilized a structured athletic activity prior to refreshments and discussion with early adolescents. Sands and Golub (1974) developed a model that utilized talking as the basic medium and group process as the material of therapy and basic group intervention during 16-week sessions. Lewis and Weinstein (1978) specifically focused on learning friendship skills with latency-age children for 5 weeks, meeting twice a week. Charach (1983) experimented with a six-session interpretive psychotherapy group.

COMPARISONS

Few efforts have been made to organize and compare the different models of group therapy for children and adolescents. MacLennan (1977) describes limitations and adaptations of classical activity group therapy due to population, setting, and service differences, classifying other models of group therapy accordingly. Schamess (1976) attempts to clear the confusion by focusing on differing diagnoses, including level of pathology and ego organization, as the decisive factor in treatment plan and group structure. He categorized existing group therapy models into four diagnostic groupings.

STAGE MODELS OF GROUP DEVELOPMENT

Although there is an abundance of literature on stage models of group development, these models have largely been formulated with adult populations. Three very different noteworthy articles exist surveying, comparing, and classifying this literature (Braaten, 1974/1975; Tuckman, 1965; Whittaker, 1970). This literature supports a substantial consensus and inherent order regarding developmental group-process models. The models compared range from 2 to 13 phases, with the larger numbers including subphasing and transitional phases.

The Sarri and Galinsky model (1974), although derived from research, is worthy of mention, as it not only posits phases of development but outlines a treatment sequence that includes therapist techniques and interventions for concurrent stages of treatment. During the origin phase, a pregroup stage, the therapist does intake, selection, and diagnosis. The therapist concentrates on group formation during the formative phase. The intermediate phase I finds the therapist building a viable and cohesive group. He or she maintains the group through the revision phase and guides group process toward treatment goals during the intermediate phase II. The therapist maintains the group through the maturation phase and terminates the group in the termination phase.

The Garland, Jones, and Kolodny model (1973) has been the only group developmental model specifically conceived for and illustrated with children's groups. Developed under Bernstein at the Boston School of Social Work, this model is based on the assumptions that closeness is the central theme in the process and development of groups, that a frame of reference can be employed for perception and behavior, and that this changes as the character of the group changes. Formulating a conceptual outline for the tasks, process, and structure of the group helps provide a normative structure of healthy, normal processes. This model is felt to be most complete by Whittaker and has many similarities with that of this book's authors. The worker focus and intervention material is solid and excellent. The five-stage model begins with preaffiliation and the early struggle of approach-avoidance of initial closeness. Power and control issues surface in the second stage, forming largely on the worker-group relationship. Stage three, intimacy, is characterized by more intense involvement and openness of feelings. Differentiation follows as members accept and evaluate each other and the group experience as unique and distinct. Group and individual identity are heightened during this phase of cohesion. The last stage, separation, brings with it regression and recapitulation.

Children's group psychotherapists, recognizing and labeling group phases, but not proposing stage theories, are Anthony, Karson, Schiffer, and Sugar. Anthony (1973) distinguishes three phases of treatment; the initial, intermediate, and terminal. Karson (1965) also describes three phases. The first, lasting six to nine sessions, is spent testing limits and utilizing play to express feelings. Phase two, lasting twice as long, consists of working through or redirecting hostile impulses into sublimatory channels. This is accomplished through the medium of model construction. The last phase includes encouragement to plan activities and deal with termination.

Schiffer (1969) labels four psychodynamic group process phases that are based on the interaction between the children and the worker and are evolutionary, following an "elastic time-table." During the preparatory phase, reaction is largely to the worker's permissiveness, learning and testing its realities, which lasts approximately six sessions. The longest in duration, the therapeutic phase, sees the development of the transference on multiple levels, including regressions, aggressions, catharsis, and abatement of anxiety and guilt. The reeducational phase evidences increased frustration tolerance, the capacity for delaying gratification, sublimation, improved self-image, more reality-oriented identifications, successful group interaction and responsiveness, and more efficient group controls. Separation anxiety causes temporary regression prior to acceptance during the termination phase.

Sugar (1974) recognizes three phases of group treatment. The initial phase, lasting 6 to 15 sessions, moves the child from a state of isolation through anxiety, resistance, and avoidance to some cohesion and stability in group dynamics. The middle phase reveals the group emerging, talking about problems with one another, revealing more dependency, and showing identification—functioning as a cohesive, working group. This phase lasts from 3 months to 3 years, after which the child's functioning has improved and he can relate well. The termination phase lasts from 3 weeks to 3 months, with both the child and the group sharing sadness and separation anxiety.

CHALLENGES

Scheidlinger (1968) reflected that in the 1940s children's group therapy had been a "major sphere of clinical practice" led by the "leading pioneers" (p. 445). The field has heavily concentrated on Slavson's models and their modification, with much restatement of original theory. Redl and Anthony also have had an impact, focusing issues of the therapist's role and group process orientation. The field has lost momentum and some of its greats, even since the 1960s. Anthony, Durkin, Redl, and Scheidlinger have not continued to advance theoretical and clinical developments in the field because of other pursuits. Slavson and Ginott have passed away. In the 1970s and 1980s new theoretical developments have been reflected in children's and adolescents' group therapy. These are in developmental psychology (Frank), object relations theory (Trafimow, Levin), and peer relations theory (Grunebaum & Solomon, 1980, 1982).

A challenge is evident because of the paucity of literature in several areas. Reference is made to inadequate or nonexistent training programs as an aside, with none being presented directly or in detail. This area is important, since it is clear that the qualifications and kinds of demands are different with children and adolescents and in some cases greater than they are with adults. Discussion of supervision, co-therapy, and transference/countertransference issues are of utmost importance yet almost nonexistent in the children's and adolescents' literature. Group dynamics and group developmental models also are scarce. Little is available on the internal and external processes the group therapist experiences, the multidimensional relationships inherent in these groups, and the parallel processes. This volume is an attempt to address these issues.

As it is most unlikely that any one theoretical and clinical model will encompass all types of children and adolescents in all settings, there is room for models to be developed with varying orientations, goals, and techniques. In 1971 Kraft stated that a therapist "should be exposed to several theories from which he can evolve both a pragmatic self-fit for work and a vocabulary to describe what transpires. From the theories and from his supervised experiences, he produces an individualized therapeutic style that enables him to work well and comfortably with his patients" (p. 636).

Serious challenges still face the field. As Kaplan and Sadock (1971) have observed, "few therapists have been trained for or are willing to undertake the group treatment of children and adolescents" (p. 516). There are losses to the field every day of both learners and leaders due to other priorities or to the difficulty and unpopularity of these groups. There is too often a lack of peer understanding and support and a lack of training and supervision. These are extremely important because of the high personal and professional demands on the therapist inherent in leading these groups. Greater responsibility remains with those continuing to teach and practice in the field. More meetings need to be held in professional organizations, with perhaps a group identification and recognition of needs. Studies of group practice with children and adolescents are needed, not just from a historical perspective but including who, where, and what models are being practiced, where training exists, and why there is not more publishing and advancement of theory.

REFERENCES

Anthony, E. J. (1973). Group-analytic psychotherapy with children and adolescents. In S. H. Foulkes & E. J. Anthony (Eds.), *Group psychotherapy: The psychoanalytic approach* (rev. 2nd ed.). Baltimore: Penguin Books. pp. 186–232.

Appley, D. G., & Winder, A. E. (1973). *T-groups and therapy groups in a changing society.* San Francisco: Jossey-Bass.

Axline, M. (1947). *Play therapy.* Boston: Houghton Mifflin.

Barcai, A., & Robinson, E. H. (1969). Conventional group therapy with preadolescent children. *International Journal of Group Psychotherapy, 19,* 334–345.

Berkovitz, I. H. (Ed.). (1972). *Adolescents grow in groups: Experiences in adolescent group psychotherapy.* New York: Brunner/Mazel.

Blotcky, M. J., Scheinbein, M., Wiggins, K. M., & Forgotson, J. H. (1980). A verbal group technique for ego-disturbed children: Action to words. *International Journal of Psychoanalytic Psychotherapy, 81,* 203–232.

Braaten, L. J. (1974/1975). Developmental phases of encounter groups and related intensive groups. *Interpersonal Development, 5,* 112–129.

Brandes, N. S., & Gardner, M. L. (Eds.). (1973). *Group therapy for the adolescent.* New York: Jason Aronson.

Charach, R. (1983). Brief interpretive group psychotherapy with early latency-age children. *International Journal of Group Psychotherapy, 33,* 349–364.

Durkin, H. E. (1939). Dr. John Levy's relationship therapy as applied to a play group. *American Journal of Orthopsychiatry, 9,* 583–597.

Epstein, N. & Altman, S. (1972). Experiences in converting an activity therapy group into verbal group therapy with latency-age boys. *International Journal of Group Psychotherapy, 22,* 93–100.

Frank, M. G. (1976). Modifications of activity group therapy: Responses to ego-impoverished children. *Clinical Social Work Journal, 4,* 102–109.

Frank, M. G., & Zilbach, J. (1968). Current trends in group therapy with children. *International Journal of Group Psychotherapy, 18,* 447–460.

Gabriel, B. (1939). An experiment in group treatment. *American Journal of Orthopsychiatry, 9,* 146–169.

Ganter, G., Yeakel, M., & Polansky, N. A. (1967). *Retrieval from limbo: The intermediary group treatment of inaccessible children.* New York: Child Welfare League of America.

Garland, J. A., Jones, H. E., & Kolodny, R. L. (1973). A model for stages of development in social work groups. In S. Bernstein (Ed.). *Explorations in group work: Essays in theory and practice.* Boston: Milford House. pp. 17–71.

Ginott, H. G. (1961). *Group psychotherapy with children.* New York: McGraw-Hill.

Glatzer, H. T., & Durkin, H. E. (1944). The role of the therapist in group relationship therapy. *The Nervous Child, 4,* 243–251.

Gratton, L., & Pope, L. (1972). Group diagnosis and therapy for young school children. *Hospital and Community Psychiatry, 23,* 180–200.

Gratton, L., & Rizzo, A. E. (1969). Group therapy with young psychotic children. *International Journal of Group Psychotherapy, 19,* 63–71.

Grunebaum, H., & Solomon, L. (1980). Toward a peer theory of group psychotherapy: 1. On the developmental significance of peers and play. *International Journal of Group Psychotherapy, 30,* 23–49.

Grunebaum, H., & Solomon, L. (1982). Toward a theory of peer relationships: 2. On the stages of social development and their relationship to group psychotherapy. *International Journal of Group Psychotherapy, 32,* 283–307.

Kaplan, H. I., & Sadock, B. J. (Eds.). (1971). *Comprehensive group psychotherapy.* Baltimore: Williams & Wilkins.

Karson, S. (1965). Group psychotherapy with latency age boys. *International Journal of Group Psychotherapy, 15,* 81–89.

Kraft, I. A. (1971). Child and adolescent group psychotherapy. In H. I. Kaplan & B. J. Sadock (Eds.), *Comprehensive group psychotherapy.* Baltimore: Williams & Wilkins. pp. 534–565.

Levin, S. (1982). The adolescent group as transitional object. *International Journal of Group Psychotherapy, 32,* 217–232.

Lewis, K., & Weinstein, L. (1978). Friendship skills: Intense short-term intervention with latency age children. *Social Work with Groups, 1,* 279–286.

Lifton, N., & Smolen, E. M. (1966). Group psychotherapy with schizophrenic children. *International Journal of Group Psychotherapy, 16,* 131–141.

Lowrey, L. G. (1944). Group treatment for mothers. *American Journal of Orthopsychiatry, 14,* 589–592.

Lubin, B., & Lubin, A. W. (1973). The group psychotherapy literature 1972. *International Journal of Group Psychotherapy, 23,* 474–513.

Lubin, B., Lubin, A. W., & Sargent, C. W. (1972). The group psychotherapy literature 1971. *International Journal of Group Psychotherapy, 22,* 492–529.

MacLennan, B. W. (1977). Modifications of activity group therapy for children. *International Journal of Group Psychotherapy, 27,* 85–96.

MacLennan, B. W., & Felsenfeld, N. (1968). *Group counseling and psychotherapy with adolescents.* New York: Columbia University Press.

MacLennan, B. W., & Levy, N. (1967). The group psychotherapy literature 1966. *International Journal of Group Psychotherapy, 17,* 378–398.

MacLennan, B. W., & Levy, N. (1968). The group psychotherapy literature 1967. *International Journal of Group Psychotherapy, 18,* 375–401.

MacLennan, B. W., & Levy, N. (1969). The group psychotherapy literature 1968. *International Journal of Group Psychotherapy, 19,* 382–408.

MacLennan, B. W., & Levy, N. (1970). The group psychotherapy literature 1969. *International Journal of Group Psychotherapy, 20,* 380–411.

MacLennan, B. W., & Levy, N. (1971). The group psychotherapy literature 1970. *International Journal of Group Psychotherapy, 21,* 345–380.

Pelosi, A. A., & Friedman, H. (1974). The activity period in group psychotherapy. *Psychiatric Quarterly, 48,* 223–229.

Rachman, A. W. (1975). *Identity group psychotherapy with adolescents.* Springfield, IL: Charles C Thomas.

Redl, F. (1942). Group emotion and leadership. *Psychiatry, 5,* 573–596.

Redl, F. (1949). The phenomenon of contagion and "shock effect." In K. R. Eissler (Ed.), *Searchlights in delinquency.* New York: International Universities Press. pp. 315–328.

Redl, F. (1966). *When we deal with children.* New York: Free Press.

Redl, F., & Wineman, D. (1957). *The aggressive child* New York: Free Press.

Rhodes, S. L. (1973). Short-term groups of latency-age children in a school setting. *International Journal of Group Psychotherapy, 23,* 204–216.

Rose, S. D. (1972). *Treating children in groups: A behavioral approach.* San Francisco: Jossey-Bass.

Rosenbaum, M., & Kraft, I. A. (1975). Group psychotherapy for children. In M. Rosenbaum & M. M. Berger (Eds.), *Group psychotherapy and group function* (rev. ed.). New York: Basic Books. pp. 588–607.

Sands, R. M., & Golub, S. (1974). Breaking the bonds of tradition: A reassessment of group treatment of latency-age children. *American Journal of Psychiatry, 131,* 662–665.

Sarri, R. C., & Galinsky, M. J. (1974). A conceptual framework for group development. In P. Glasser, R. Sarri, & R. Vinter (Eds.), *Individual change through small groups.* New York: Free Press. pp. 71–88.

Schachter, R. S. (1974). Kinetic psychotherapy in the treatment of children. *American Journal of Psychotherapy, 28,* 430–437.

Schachter, R. S. (1984). Kinetic psychotherapy in the treatment of depression in latency age children. *International Journal of Group Psychotherapy, 34,* 83–91.

Schamess, G. (1976). Group treatment modalities for latency-age children. *International Journal of Group Psychotherapy, 26,* 455–473.

Scheidlinger, S. (1960). Experimental group treatment of severely deprived latency age children. *American Journal of Orthopsychiatry, 30,* 356–368.

Scheidlinger, S. (1965). Three approaches with socially deprived latency age children. *International Journal of Group Psychotherapy, 15,* 434–445.

Scheidlinger, S. (1968). Current trends in group therapy with children and adolescents: Introductory remarks. *International Journal of Group Psychotherapy, 18,* 445–446.

Schiffer, M. (1969). *Therapeutic play group.* New York: Grune & Stratton.

Schiffer, M. (1977). Activity-interview group psychotherapy: Theory, principles, and practice. *International Journal of Group Psychotherapy, 27,* 377–388.

Slavson, S. R. (1943). *An introduction to group therapy.* New York: International Universities Press.

Slavson, S. R. (1945). Differential methods of group therapy in relation to age levels. *The Nervous Child, 4,* 196–209.

Slavson, S. R. (1947). Differential dynamics of activity and interview group therapy. *American Journal of Orthopsychiatry, 17,* 293–302.

Slavson, S. R., & Schiffer, M. (1975). *Group psychotherapies for children.* New York: International Universities Press.

Speers, R. W., & Lansing, C. (1965). *Group therapy in childhood psychoses.* Chapel Hill, NC: University of North Carolina Press.

Strunk, C. S., & Witkin, L. J. (1974). The transformation of a latency-age girls group from unstructured play to problem-focused discussion. *International Journal of Group Psychotherapy, 24,* 460–470.

Sugar, M. (1974). Interpretive group psychotherapy with latency children. *Journal of the American Academy of Child Psychiatry, 13,* 648–666.

Sugar, M. (Ed.). (1975). *The adolescent in group and family therapy.* New York: Brunner/Mazel.

Trafimow, E., & Pattak, S. I. (1981). Group psychotherapy and objectal development in children. *International Journal of Group Psychotherapy, 31,* 193–204.

Trafimow, E., & Pattak, S. I. (1982). Group treatment of primitively fixated children. *International Journal of Group Psychotherapy, 32*, 445–452.

Tuckman, B. W. (1965). Developmental sequences in groups. *Psychological Bulletin, 63*, 384–399.

VanScoy, H. (1971). An activity group approach to severely disturbed latency boys. *Child Welfare, 50*, 413–419.

Whittaker, J. K. (1970). Models of group development. *Social Service Review, 4*, 308–322.

Chapter 3

STAGE I: PREPARATION

Margot Schnitzer de Neuhaus

Experiential Description

Someone comes up with the idea of having a group. As the word spreads throughout the agency, staff members react with varying degrees of interest, some secretly hoping it will turn out to be a fantasy, while others are curious about the possibilities and consequences of carrying out such an idea. The secretaries speculate about the number of letters, appointment slips, and calls the group would entail, while the receptionist anxiously anticipates a problem controlling a group of "those kids" while they wait for the group to begin. Administrators warn about disruption of "the proper working atmosphere" and the degree of property damage that a group of unruly and noisy children could inflict, always cognizant of the image portrayed to the Director or the Board.

There are clinical staff skeptical about the idea, those strongly opposed often from individual treatment orientations. "Just because group therapy is different, everybody wants to try it. Are we going to allow our staff to submit to the pressures of treating more, faster, and less frequently, in hopes of better results and/or cutting costs? What has become of the traditional treatment with proven effectiveness? Is there anyone trained to conduct these groups who really knows what they are doing? Who would supervise? What about getting the appropriate room and equipment? Coordinating all of that seems impractical, expensive, and confusing! What parent would want to entrust his child to an agency that would only compound his problems by putting him in a room full of others just like him or worse? Just imagine the noise! What will happen to the agency's reputation?"

On the other hand, there are some clinical staff members who have experienced the effectiveness of groups. Among them are the family therapists and the therapists with some group training or group experience. These are the ones who promote group therapy with considerably more enthusiasm. "It's about time! I have a number of patients who could use group therapy, some who could use it in addition to individual treatment. Who will be the therapist? I'm not sure that I could do it now, not with my tight schedule; though it would be interesting to try. Maybe grouping some of my patients together I could participate in some real changes around here." The first wave of vague rumblings and rumors moves through the agency and subsides when everyone is somewhat aware of his colleagues' thoughts on the issue. Beginning at this point, a more vigorous second wave moves toward the higher echelons with openly verbalized questions: "Are we really going to have a group?" "Who's going to lead it?" "Can we hire a group expert?" Finally, the response from the administration; "Yes, we will have a group." "Is there a volunteer therapist?" There is mild panic, a disorganized reorganization of attitudes. Emerging from this confusion, a group therapist is appointed or has somehow volunteered.

In his attempt to gather himself and his material together, the newly identified group therapist can be seen scurrying around the clerical area. The secretaries, in turn, are seen frantically shuffling papers in an attempt to accommodate his seemingly endless requests for information. On his way back to his office, he is stopped by his colleague: "I hear you are running *The Group.*" The idea has become reality with a title. They either offer help or express their condolences for his new assignment, their remarks often providing a moment of comic relief. It

serves as a startling reminder that he is in new territory, experiencing mixed feelings, and sometimes fumbling for words, not
knowing quite how to verbalize his goals for the group. The
therapist tries to remain calm, returns to his office, and calls his
co-therapist. He or they focus on what kind of a group it will be,
turning to the literature and a supervisor to help find direction
and ease anxiety.

After careful consideration, the therapist emerges from his
office, having formulated some formal guidelines, and directs
himself to the intake worker and the rest of the staff to request
referrals. Reviewing the referrals, the therapist selects cases that
seem most appropriate. He calls or writes to them, and if they
show interest in participating, he schedules an appointment.
The administration relinquishes a room, hoping that the therapist keeps the children confined to it and that he quickly instills
in them respect for the room and its contents and agency rules.
As the clerical procedures are completed and interviews with
prospective group members take place, everyone begins to accept the group as part of the agency's program.

Parents who have been contacted also experience confused
and mixed thoughts and feelings. "They said Mark might benefit from the group. Does that mean he's in really bad shape or
that he's not so bad after all? I know he fights with everyone, but
does that mean he needs a group? Who knows what kind of kids
would come to the group from that neighborhood? Boy, I'd like
to see the person who thinks he can handle my kid and five others like him! The idea of putting all of them in one room at the
same time! They'd probably come out worse. Maybe that therapist will turn my child against me. Maybe this won't be good for
him after all. But the school and our neighbor have said it's a
good place and it can help. I guess I'll go hear what they have to
say and then make up my mind. Maybe Mark won't feel so left
out and different. It actually makes more sense than seeing him
alone, as his problems only show up when he's around other
kids."

At the same time, the child may be thinking and feeling:
"Kids like me in a group, huh? I haven't seen anybody like me
yet! I can't just tell anybody what's on my mind; they'd probably

not understand and might even make fun of me. It'd turn out like it always does; the kids would do something rotten, I'd have to do something about it, and then I'd get into trouble for it. I'm getting tired of feeling so messed up. I've tried to forget about it, but it just seems to be getting worse. I have no friends and those grown-ups are constantly on my back. Maybe I do need help. My counselor in school thinks a group would be good for me. I wonder if the group therapist will talk straight like my counselor? If he finds out what I'm really like, he just might get scared to death and quit, or worse yet, decide he doesn't like me. Maybe they'll have snacks and the boy next to me will become my friend. Perhaps it would be easier to talk with other kids who are like me and could understand. Adults don't really, and I've had enough grown-ups' answers. I want kids' answers. I'll go see what he has to say."

The idea of the existence of a group reaches a startling concreteness as soon as the screening interviews begin. Dealing with becoming a group member, the child's and parents' feelings become acute. After interviewing many potential group members, the therapist reviews the names of suitable candidates, coming up with a combination that might be motivated and compatible. As he selects the children he also takes into consideration the degree of commitment to the treatment process of the parents and of each child. Now that the preliminary work is behind him, he is relieved and eager to begin. "I wish I could start right away. It seems like a nice bunch of kids. It's going to be interesting and fun. I'd better ask the secretary to send the appointment slips for the first meeting. I wish I had a two-week vacation between now and then!"

Concurrently, the parents are nervous and concerned about how their child will fare in the group; the child may be thinking what he will wear the first day. "I wonder who will be in the group and if they will like me?"

The day of the first session has arrived. The children, parents, and even the therapist did not sleep well the night before, as they mulled over their fantasies and fears about the new group. They are nervous and impatient as they get ready for their appearance at the agreed time and place.

DYNAMIC DESCRIPTION

The *preparation stage* is an integral and crucial part of the process and outcome of group therapy. Most stage theories in the literature usually begin with the first session. A notable exception to this in the practice literature is Sarri and Galinsky's (1974) model of group therapy. They include a pregroup stage, origin phase, covering the period of intake, selection, and diagnosis. Our stage covers a similar period, beginning with the inception of the idea of the group up until the first session. Braaten (1974/1975) in his composite model also included a pregroup phase.

Conceptualizing, screening, composing, and balancing the group are the important tasks that must be accomplished by the therapist during the preparation stage. The stage conveniently divides into three conceptual phases. The first encompasses the preparatory efforts made by the agency in establishing a group treatment program. It begins with the inception of the idea of group psychotherapy, including the decision-making process, through the arrangement of administrative and clerical details that precede the functioning of the group, up to and including the selection of the group therapist.

The second phase entails the therapist's preparatory efforts in becoming the group therapist of this group. This preparation is emotional as well as intellectual and practical. First he establishes his position vis-a-vis the group in terms of his capacities, preferences, objectives, and treatment orientation; then he selects and defines the composition of the group. He takes into consideration his role and the agency needs and expectations.

The third phase pertains to the child's and the parents' preparatory efforts in becoming participants in the group treatment program. It includes the screening process to select the appropriate candidates who would form a working, well-balanced group. This phase also includes an explanation by the therapist to the parents and child of the conditions necessary for group treatment to take place, including the portion of the work to be done by each. It also establishes the beginning of the trusting relationship between the child, his parents, and the therapist. This relationship serves as a bridge for the child to the group and to all future relationships within the group. The relationship provides the parents with guidance and support in allowing their child to undergo the treatment process.

Clearly, the work accomplished during this stage affects the readiness of the agency to have groups, of the therapist to conduct group therapy, of the group composition to be balanced yet dynamic, of the group candidates to undergo the group treatment, and of the parents to allow their children to do so.

The Agency

Agencies providing clinical or psychiatric services for children and adolescents at some point consider the issues involved in including group therapy as a treatment modality. This consideration may be motivated by administrative or clinical staff, internal service demands, a decrease in staff and funding, and/or outside community pressure. The agency's characteristic decision-making patterns in the establishment and carrying out of procedures and programs will be evident again in this process of considering and forming groups. In addition to agency setting, funding, and population served, agency theoretical orientation, training commitments, staffing structures, diagnostic and treatment services, and physical facility influence the type of group, composition, goals, duration, and staff hired.

Consideration involves pros and cons. Some inconveniences result from a group of five to seven children; noisier halls, greater risk of property damage, difficulty with control, additional clerical and staff time, special supplies, equipment, and room. Often there is general agency upheaval, and personnel with special skills are necessary. On the other hand, some children's problems are better serviced through group therapy, and it can augment other treatment modalities. In addition, a more flexible, comprehensive service can be provided. Often shorter waits for service and favorable economic conditions are achieved by running groups.

The agency is responsible for providing a climate supportive of and conducive to successful groups. This includes selecting and training the group therapist; providing supportive backup clinical services, such as diagnostic evaluation, individual

treatment, parental treatment, and staff available to handle crises as necessary; supportive clerical and maintenance staff; pro-
vision of equipment, room, and house rules.

When the agency is physically and psychologically prepared
to tolerate the noise and stress, the therapist and children are
not placed under as great a strain. In most settings it is helpful to
have a cooling-off place in the hall and/or a time-out, quiet, or
freedom room where the child can safely regain control and
then be able to return to the room to continue therapeutic work.
Unless there are co-therapists, and even sometimes when there
are, another worker will need to be trained and used to help
man the hall or quiet room. This may be a child care worker,
nurse's aide, milieu worker, volunteer, or another staff member
who makes himself or herself available during the group time.
The person who monitors the hall is responsible for watching
the child and not leaving him or her alone, but the therapist
must be involved in placing the child in the room, along with
dealing with the child's feelings and again with handling them
once the child has returned to the group room.

When a positive, accepting attitude toward group psychotherapy is adopted by the agency administration, it has a great
impact on the attitude of the rest of the staff. They feel supported in their struggles with the changes necessary when
groups are formed. Adequate communication, trust, and good
will among administrators, staff, and therapist help in the understanding of the parallel processes that are played out during
the duration of the group as it passes through various stages.

Sometimes in addition to the support the agency supplies,
the therapist must work specifically with colleagues and ancillary
staff, listening to their fears and concerns, providing enough
understanding and support for them to be able to carry out their
portion of the responsibilities to the group. Staff can be interested in fulfilling their roles in getting the group started or they
can resist, procrastinate, and even sabotage the therapist's efforts. At times colleagues may not make referrals or they may be
grossly inappropriate; appointment slips may not be sent or
equipment not ordered. Sometimes the therapist must do as
much education and preparation of the staff as he does of the

children and parents to ensure a smooth and successful beginning and progression of the group.

Kadis, Krasner, Winick, and Foulkes (1963) also stress preparation of all personnel responsible for and having a part in the implementation of group therapy programs in order to ensure initial and ongoing cooperation. In institutional settings where a clear hierarchy exists, "the group therapy program may do much to dispel sources of staff conflict and tension. It unites professionals of various backgrounds, . . . facilitates communication . . . and may tend to enhance mutual trust" (Kadis et al., 1963, p. 26). When it offends or threatens certain staff, this can often be "overcome with the passage of time and education" (Kadis et al., p. 26).

Barcai and Robinson (1969) highlight the importance of agency atmosphere and degree of cooperation in their comparison study in two different schools. In one school, where administration appeared concerned with discipline, frustrations and impediments were repeatedly present, and it was felt that underlying messages had been transmitted and had affected the children's response to therapy (p. 344).

The Therapist

Ambivalence is experienced by all group therapists. The range and intensity of the therapist's affect varies according to character structure, amount of experience, and motivation for assuming the responsibility. Vacillating between feelings of enthusiasm and expectation, fear of personal or professional failure, anxiety and varying degrees of panic, each therapist utilizes defense mechanisms common to his or her personality structure to deal with these intense feelings. If the therapist has been coerced into running the group, he or she must deal with any anger or resentment present so that unresolved feelings do not interfere with a successful outcome.

While forming the group, the therapist has several issues to consider and decisions to make. These involve personal and professional interests as well as characteristics specific to this group. Personally, he or she may feel motivated to run a group because of curiosity, challenge, growth experience, and intellectual knowledge. Professionally, the therapist may want to further his or her experience by experimenting with different group therapy models, types of populations, groupings, goals, techniques, and/or co-therapy. After considering these preferences, the therapist must consider and choose a theoretical orientation, treatment approach, group composition, and treatment goals. Certain "given" characteristics, such as agency population, as defined by geographical location, economic, and ethnic backgrounds, as well as severity and manifestation of disturbance, must also be considered. Other practical givens include the agency's clinical requirements, definition of the therapist's role, and availability of an appropriate room.

Through self-searching and discussion with colleagues, supervisor, and co-therapist, the therapist balances these professional, personal, and practical considerations. With an effort to maintain consistency of theoretical framework, technique, composition, and goals, the therapist emerges with a set of guidelines. Prospective group candidates are evaluated in terms of these in order to choose children who would appear to benefit most from this group.

The screening interviews are taxing due to their dual purpose, assessing and educating the prospective members. Considerable skill, experience, and intuition is helpful in selecting, composing, and balancing the group. Pressure is felt to avoid making a wrong decision, which could mean leaving out a child who should have been included, or including one who would later prove to be inappropriate. Such mistakes are made and are reparable, but they also are painful for all of those involved. In spite of the care and time taken in choosing the group members, the therapist does not "really know" how the child and group are going to function until the group has begun to meet. He or she often has to change goals and guidelines, compromising original expectations and hopes. The therapist must resolve his or her feelings regarding these changes so that they do not interfere with the treatment.

After selecting the children, choosing the room, deciding on the inclusion or exclusion of refreshments, toys, games, and activities, the therapist completes the necessary administrative and clerical details. Even if the therapist does not have the full quota of children by the time the group is scheduled to begin, he or she may choose to begin, telling the children one or two may enter the group later. At some point during this lengthy process, his or her role as group therapist has become accepted and internalized. He or she is now *The Group Therapist*, the group is *his* (or her) *group*, and he or she is ready to begin.

The Parents

The feelings parents experience as they contact the agency depend on their motivation for seeking treatment. Their feelings are affected by their level of awareness of the problem, their desire and capacity to change, and their ambivalence. Some parents who appear motivated for their child to get help may be merely projecting their own problems onto the child. They may be overly identified with their child or cannot face their own difficulties. These parents may lose interest in the treatment or sabotage it once the child begins to change. Ideally, these parents need a strong therapeutic relationship for themselves from the beginning of their child's treatment for them to allow their child to remain for the duration of the group.

All parents are ambivalent at a conscious or unconscious level of awareness, sincerely wanting to do what is best for their child, at the same time sensing that obtaining this necessitates change, a feared unknown. Fearing change and confrontation of painful hidden issues, their patterns of denial further reinforce avoidance. The therapist helps these parents confront their ambivalence. If their child is selected for the group, these parents may need some form of therapy throughout the group's duration to ensure they do not sabotage the treatment.

Both at this early stage and throughout treatment, common questions and reactions are: What is the cause of the problem, what is the therapeutic process, and what is the expected outcome? This questioning is similar to that of individual psychotherapy. Realizing the need for more help than they have given, parents question their effectiveness, wondering if they are to blame. They see themselves as good parents, loving and caring, having made repeated efforts to raise their child "the right way."

They are guilty about all the times they may have overreacted, hit when they should not have, and yelled when they should have understood. Confused and vacillating in their reactions, they may fear an innate or acquired "badness," "meanness," or "craziness" in themselves and/or their child. They wonder, "Will I recognize my child when it's over? Will you turn my child against me?" They want relief but fear disharmony, loss, and even their inability to change. This new experience needs guidelines and ways to begin trusting, as they often fear rejection and criticism. How successful the therapist is in gaining their support and trust will profoundly influence the entire treatment process. Parents at this stage are equally as important as the children.

In spite of the therapist's caution and preparation, some parents get so confused and overwhelmed that they are unable to hear answers and accept emotional support. They resist further involvement, dropping out because they sense they are not ready or able to handle this complex and difficult process. All parents resist dealing with parts of the process at one time or another. If only a few questions surface at this stage, these and others need to be confronted later in order to deal with resistances and to ensure the parents' continued cooperation. Parents need differing amounts of help and emotional support.

The Child

Sometimes the child has not been told the reasons for the screening interview and may have just heard about the group. Regardless of what he has been told, he feels anxiety and senses it in his parents. The range of fantasies and feelings he experiences may be distorted, due to nonverbal and verbal messages and feelings he received from his parents, peers, and community. His internal concept of himself as possibly being "sick," "bad," "mental," or "crazy" is affecting him. As he is faced with the reality of the interview, he may be experiencing and may show any combination of fear, anger, panic, frustration, denial, resistance, embarrassment, shame, guilt, and relief.

Throughout the screening interview, shifts in the child's responsiveness may be evident as intense ambivalent feelings and resistances surface. The child handles these with defense mechanisms characteristic of his or her personality structure. A highly anxious child may hear little of the interview. However, usually a child is able to grasp at least the essence, understanding that the group is being planned and that he or she is being considered for it.

At this point a child may want nothing further to do with becoming a member of the group. That child may feel threatened and wish to flee or simply may be not interested in a group but will ask about the other treatment modalities. Another child may want what the group seems to promise, feeling relieved and calmed as he or she stays and hears more. Such children will then attempt to formulate the problems that they feel need help. Children converting their difficulties into action will need help in verbalization, as may children who have had no previous treatment. At the end of this interview the therapist informs the child and parents whether the child would benefit from group therapy. Whether or not he or she is accepted for the group, the child will respond with ambivalence. The child needs to understand the reasons for the outcome and needs preparation for whatever lies ahead.

SPECIAL ISSUES

The issues in this section are delicately and intricately related. They are the first steps taken in establishing the therapeutic communication and relationship-oriented focus.

Group Selection and Composition

The selection of the group theory and model, size and members, must follow a consistently integrated pattern. It is first in the art of group psychotherapy and relies heavily on intuition and experience. Guidelines in the practice literature are confusing, difficult to compare, and sometimes contradictory. These two inextricable issues will be handled together in an attempt to clarify and highlight.

Ideally, the therapist has control over the type of group chosen and the membership. Factors contributing to this choice include the therapist's training and professional motivations. Much of the format of the group is inherent in the choice of theory and model. Goals, techniques, size, composition, duration, frequency of sessions, and room are integrally related to these theoretical approaches and cannot be handled separately.

Yalom (1970) reviews the literature on selection criteria in adult groups and comments on the lack of consensus, highly individualized terminology, contradictions, and scarcity of guidelines. More exclusion (brain damage, paranoia, extreme narcissism, hypochondriasis, suicide, addiction, acute psychosis, sociopathism) than inclusion criteria are presented. There is a clinical consensus that exclusion should be on the basis of the patient's inability to participate in the primary task of the group, that is, to relate to other group members. Yalom's study identified two variables predicting success; a patient's attraction to the group and a patient's general popularity in the group, which seems related to his high degree of self-disclosure and ability to introspect. The therapist's positive personal feelings toward the patient also were determined to correlate with success. Yalom further states that if change is to occur, compatibility must exist between the patient and the interpersonal need culture of the group and that cohesiveness must be the primary guideline utilized in selection. In other words, individual selection should be based on the lowest likelihood of premature termination, and the group must be balanced for the greatest likelihood of cohesion.

In the children's group literature one finds listings of clinical and characterological traits of children that are indicated and contraindicated for various types of group therapy (Ginott, 1961; Slavson, 1955). Peck and Stewart's (1964) survey of playgroup therapy in child treatment facilities, reported 77 percent of the responders had exclusion criteria. Nearly all considered age and sex as indispensable variables, 76 percent considered intellectual level important, and 68 percent considered diagnostic classification and dynamics as important. The most frequent practice was heterogeneous grouping by dynamics, "but the ability to interact with others was considered to supercede this consideration" (Peck & Stewart, 1964, p. 146).

Bertcher and Maple (1974) and Rose (1972) are of the belief

that behavioral attributes are better predictors of individual behavior in groups than are descriptive attributes such as age and
sex. The behavioral attributes are the ways a child acts or is expected to act based on his or her past performance. The critical
attributes the group therapist is looking for depends on the
group objectives and development. Rose ranks behavioral assets
and deficits on a scale from 1 to 10 and will place a child in a
group only if another is near him on most continua (pp. 23–24).
Bertcher and Maple have devised a more elaborate method of
ranking and charting these attributes on a linear continuum,
with plusses and minuses, allowing for decisions regarding composition to be done almost arithmetically. They find greater
comfort is experienced if descriptive attributes are similar. Yet
too much compatibility makes a group ineffective, as does too
much stress, inadequate identification models, and negative subgroups. Therefore, Bertcher and Maple present a way of choosing two children from each cluster of identified critical behavioral attributes as their way of balancing for interaction,
compatibility, and mutual responsiveness.

Along these lines, Slavson (1955) states that the chief re-
quirement for including a child in activity group therapy is the
child's desire to be a part of the group and his ability to establish
object relationships. Additionally, "he must have potential capacity to give up his undesirable behavior in return for the acceptance by the group" (p. 24), which Slavson terms social hunger. He further states that there are only two contraindications
for placement in any type of group: those that derive from inherent problems of the patient and those that may have an ad-
verse effect on each other and the group. He further states that
placement considerations require objectivity, training, and experience (p. 30). Redl and Wineman (1957) also state that a clinical
group program must be in operation for many years prior to the
development of an adequate set of criteria for selection. "Exper-
imentation with different problem intensities and types has first
to be done in order to begin to perceive clearly what the particular design has to offer to the treatment of different problem patterns found in various children" (Redl & Wineman, 1957, p. 48).

Paradise and Daniels (1976) assert that taking "needy" and
"what-is-available" children will produce groups whose outcome

is as good on the average as those more thoughtfully composed and selected (p. 37). In addition, these authors avoid utilizing diagnostic categories and caution that there are no rules, do's and don'ts, in the area of group composition. From their experience they identify 15 factors to be considered, the most important of which are developmental level, intelligence, skill, ego controls, tolerance of behavior differences, ability to communicate, ability to delay gratification, and a need to belong to "this" group (p. 44).

Charach (1983) describes the "winnowing" process occurring in clinics despite warnings as to its inadvisability. This is the practice of seeing the most promising, verbal candidates in individual treatment and the least verbal, most physically active children in group therapy. "One is far more likely to find the three most disturbed or otherwise unmanageable patients in a group than to find the three most promising children in group therapy at the same facility" (Charach, 1983, p. 351).

Only one empirical study was located that was in a residential facility for acting-out children. Johnson and Gold (1971) concluded that the selection of group members was not the crucial outcome variable but rather fitting treatment techniques to the type of children selected for the group and their behavior patterns.

The authors are in agreement with Paradise and Daniels (1976) that "composition per se is but one factor influencing the life of the group" (p. 37). The number of children who can benefit from groups is numerous and so intricately related to goals and techniques that a list of inclusions and exclusions is irrelevant and fails to provide adequate guidelines on how the child will function in the group and how these characteristics will be expressed in a group. A child should not be globally excluded from group therapy because of inappropriateness, rather "this specific group or model is inappropriate for this child for this reason." Thorough and careful placement is crucial for the outcome of treatment along with matching technique to selection to goal. Some children who would be typically excluded from groups can succeed if the group is properly selected and balanced.

Although existing models may lack in applicability and flexibility, the novice therapist is not advised to change or modify design, selection, and technique, nor to choose only partial theories or models. The therapist's strong preference for a certain diagnostic category, technique, or group structure may not be harmonious with a model he chooses. Introducing simultaneous and unknown variables affects the process, outcome, and ability to sort out issues. As a therapist gains experience, he may wish to change or modify slowly so that the unknown variables are few and can be closely observed. Many a new group has been doomed from inception because of incongruities among size, composition, theory, and technique. This harmony should exist prior to the selection of group members.

In children's group therapy practice there is considerable agreement regarding an optimal size of five to seven children dependent on the group's composition. Factors influencing the number are the age, degree of acting out, manifestation of disturbance, and existence of co-therapists. Usually a maximum of six with one therapist is recommended (Karson, 1965; Levine, 1979; Sugar, 1974). Ginott (1961) limits this to five in play group therapy with preschoolers. The authors are in agreement with Sugar that if the children are very anxious, active, aggressive, or hostile, frequently four or five is a more ideal number. Barcai and Robinson (1969) feel the larger the number of aggressive children, the smaller the group should be. If attendance problems are extreme, eight or nine children may need to be included to assure five or six being present. Karson (1965) points out a need for 10 prospects in order to select six appropriate candidates.

The two most important aspects in determining the number of children are the developmental level at which the children are functioning and the mode of expression of the children's disturbances. Often the more severely disturbed a child is found to be, the wider the discrepancy between his or her developmental level and that of his or her less disturbed chronological age mates. If the mode of expression is extremely aggressive, assaultive, hyperactive, or bizarre, such children require more attention, control, and care than those whose disturbance is expressed less violently. Size is frequently decreased by the therapist with younger children, with more severely disturbed children, with a group whose goals require specific, concentrated, and time-limited work, with a small group room, and with the therapist's self-knowledge that he feels more comfortable managing a smaller group. In contrast, the size of the group is increased by the therapist with the addition of a co-therapist, with the need to improve the group's balance, with children who are relatively intact and have internalized controls, with the necessity of meeting the agency's quota to cover expenses, and with a group whose goals are broad and open-ended.

Age spread in a group of younger children is generally 1 (Ginott) to 2 years and for latency and adolescents, up to 3 years. The span should be less if games or activities require more even skill and ability levels. Preschool can be mixed gender. Sugar and Ginott prefer same-sex groups in latency and adolescence to meet the differing developmental and social needs. Mixed-gender groups can be successfully accomplished in latency and early adolescence. It has also been our experience that strict chronological age consideration is not as important as maturity, social adjustment, school age, or developmental levels. We are in agreement with Soble and Geller (1964), that chronological age and diagnostic classification are not as important as social and emotional development of the child.

Screening

Considerable importance is placed on the process of thoughtful screening and educating of prospective group members. It is extremely helpful if the child has had a thorough diagnostic evaluation prior to the screening interview. It gives information to the therapist on the appropriateness of group therapy—that is, level of object relationships, trust, quality of friendships and peer relations, and the nature and degree of psychological and social disturbance. When dealing with a severely disturbed child, it is frequently helpful if he or she has had previous individual treatment. At times a full diagnostic evaluation should precede a recommendation for group therapy.

Without prior clinical observations and formulations the therapist must assess whether enough history and clinical material is available through the screening process to be comfortable accepting the child in a group or whether an additional diagnostic appointment is indicated. Consequently, after treatment begins, the therapist must be prepared for possible dramatic shifts in the predicted patterns of behaviors and feelings.

The purposes of the screening interview are to judge the child's motivation and capacity to engage in group treatment; to judge the parents' ability to allow the child to undergo the treatment process; to obtain a diagnostic impression of the child; and to explain to the parents and the child the function and responsibilities of the group, child, parents, and himself or herself as group therapist. The main purpose is to begin a relationship with the child so that entry into the group is easier for him or her.

The therapist begins the interview by asking what concerns the patients have and what they want of the agency, frequently asking the child first. Their answers and further exploratory work around the beginning and development of the child's problems provide the therapist with some of the information he or she is seeking. Seeing the child alone provides additional material and privacy, which frequently allows children freedom they might have lacked in their parents' presence to communicate their concerns, strengths, and weaknesses.

The therapist uses all of his or her diagnostic skills and experience in evaluating the child's appropriateness not only for group therapy but for this particular group. The questions the therapist is trying to answer are many: "Can this child see his problems as others do? Can he see his role in them? Can he identify with the feelings of others and empathize? Is he open, motivated, appropriate and willing to share of himself? Does he have flexible defenses and energy available for change and therapy? Can he delay gratifications enough to tolerate the necessity of sharing in a group? Does the child's lack of anxiety and fluidity of speech indicate few defenses or internalized controls, ego weakness or boundary problems? Will such a child out of self-preoccupation need to monpolize the therapist or the group? Could this child serve as a catalyst for the others? Will the child who is mostly silent be more communicative in a group?" Initial impressions need to be thought about and discussed with others, such as the child's therapist, his teacher, and the group consultant.

On occasion the therapist feels a need to schedule an additional interview before the group begins. He or she may assess that a more disturbed child needs extra time to establish a minimal trusting relationship with the therapist. He or she may need to see the parents again in order to insure their cooperation or because a more formal treatment contract needs to be established. However, it must be stressed that the need for these be carefully assessed with the consultant in order to prevent countertransference reactions and establishment of an individual relationship with the therapist. Experienced individual therapists but novice group therapists must be especially warned of this, which may relate to anxieties about doing group therapy. Any additional interviews should focus on preparing the child for group therapy. The therapist's need for more interviews may indicate a need for a case review, staff conference, or diagnostic evaluation before placement in a group.

Diagnostic groups have been found helpful as a part of the diagnostic process to gain peer-related information not seen or available in individual interviews (Churchill, 1965; Gratton & Pope, 1972; Redl, 1944). Even though individual screening interviews are more often utilized as predictors of group behavior, they are not especially accurate predictors of behavior exhibited in a group. This is especially the case with children who translate anxiety and issues into activity, both their own and those picked up from others in the group. Group observations can confirm or deepen other staff observations and sometimes reveal children behaving very differently in the presence of other children or with children and an adult from the way they behave when seen alone. Churchill (1965) usually sees six children in four sessions that are structured for exposure to specific stresses and social and emotional tasks. Ganter and Polansky (1964) utilize diagnostic groups to predict a child's accessibility to individual treatment. Occasionally concurrent diagnostic parent and child groups are held to gather relevant diagnostic information in place of a team diagnostic (Demsch & Brekelbaum, 1969).

The therapist is now ready to make his or her final decisions on group selection based on the results of the screening interviews. Those cases chosen for the group consist of children who are ready to work on their own problems and on the common group goals, who fit in harmony with the balancing needs of this group, and whose parents are able to allow them to engage in the treatment process.

Some groups are predetermined. If such is the case, the therapist must focus on resolving his or her own feelings about this lack of choice in order to be prepared to assume the group therapist role. If the group is inherited from a departing therapist, he or she needs to resolve his or her feelings about a group attached to and used to another therapist's style, as well as insecurities regarding his or her ability to lead a group under these circumstances. On the other hand, the therapist may rejoice in not having to make the difficult screening decisions.

Balancing

In addition to selecting and screening, the concept of balancing is widely recognized as extremely crucial in group composition. The authors utilize the term *balancing* to refer to the weighing and fitting of various physical, emotional, psychological, socioeconomic, and personality characteristics and attributes of potential group candidates, so that a dynamic and flexible equilibrium that includes tensions and differences can be established and maintained throughout the process of group therapy. To balance is to ensure the flexibility and resiliency that will enable and encourage healthy change, intimacy, achievement of goals, and successful treatment. Although abstract, balancing is all-important to the dynamic process and group growth. If a group is out of balance, it can become stagnant and unable to move away from a sometimes defensive or pathological position. A stuck group cannot progress through further stages of treatment unless membership changes or the therapist can introduce enough of a shift in structure, stimulation, or motivation to precipitate the group's movement. Group equilibrium is a dynamic, ongoing process that ebbs and flows as the group moves through the stages of group treatment. The therapist chooses the membership in an attempt to achieve this dynamic flow and continues to keep it in mind throughout the group's existence. Sometimes in later stages the therapist must introduce a change in structure or membership to re-achieve this balance.

A balancing concept is referred to by other descriptive labels by group therapists: Ginott (1961) likens it to matchmaking; Schiffer (1969), to checks and balances. Slavson (Slavson & Schiffer, 1975) has established well the concept of psychologically balanced activity groups that will foster trust, relaxational security, empathy, and achievement of a state of dynamic equilibrium. His requires a balance of behavior patterns such as positive and negative instigators, neutralizers, and neuters. Schiffer (1969) interjects that it is not enough simply to select an equal number of aggressive and withdrawn children, as there are initial qualitative differences in the nature of passive and aggressive personalities and modifications that evolve as a result of group interaction. Due to the permissive role function of the leader in this type of group, the appropriate blend of children is absolutely necessary so as to allow eventual neutralization of inappropriate behavior through self-regulation. Ginott (1961) strove for a harmonious combination that could allow optimum tension yet be a haven from persecution. He added that it should provide a diversity of identification models yet exert a corrective identification influence. Axline (1947) allowed the child to invite playmates of his own choice to make up the group. Paradise and Daniels (1973) report an imbalance occurs when the members are too similar. They seek to achieve a dynamic balance in the following areas: passive–aggressive; highly skilled–unskilled; other-oriented–self-oriented; likable–unlikable; poor reality testing–good reality testing; suggestive–resistive to contagion (p. 42).

Both homogeneous and heterogeneous groupings can be effective. With children's groups the concept of balancing has weighed heavily in favor of the peer group membership balancing itself naturally through composition. Traditionally, this has been done by balancing active and passive children. This is not possible when dealing with homogeneous populations such as acting-out, aggressive, delinquent, severely ego-impaired, psychotic, and severely socially deprived. In these groups, although some factors balance naturally, others—such as limits and con-

trol, ego and superego functions—remain the responsibility of
the therapist. By carefully structuring the group, successful experiences can be provided for these homogeneous groupings as
demonstrated by Frank (1976), Ganter, Yeakel, and Polansky
(1967), Lifton and Smolen (1966), Redl and Wineman (1957),
Scheidlinger (1960, 1965), and Speers and Lansing (1965). A
combination of tightly structuring the format and group interactions and the therapist's lending his or her ego, even at times
taking over the group ego and superego functioning, helps accomplish a successful grouping with these populations otherwise
not suited for group therapy. Other homogeneous groupings,
such as underachieving, school-phobic, or learning-disabled,
may be more loosely structured due to the presence of greater
ego controls in the children.

Homogeneous versus heterogeneous grouping is really
more of a pseudo- than an actual issue (Johnson & Gold, 1971).
More relevant issues are which factors to balance or make homogeneous (age, sex, race, diagnosis, problem, behavior, goal) and
how to use treatment techniques to work effectively with the selected children in a group. Heterogeneity in manifestation and
degree of disturbance, as well as in areas of strength and weakness is important. In their work with adults, Whitaker and Lieberman (1964) strove for a maximum of heterogeneity in the patient conflict area and pattern of coping and homogeneity in the
areas of tolerating anxiety and vulnerability.

An attempt should be made to try to ensure an interesting,
dynamic group that encourages discussion, positive identifications, and growth at many levels. It helps when children share
some common denominators, such as presenting problems,
goals, minority status, behavior, personality patterns, and group
roles. Often group balance, understanding, and appreciation of
others is enhanced when children with reverse problems or
symptoms, such as withdrawn and acting out, impulsive and inhibited, are included in the same group, as long as some children are in between. Successful balancing of composition rests
on the therapist's theoretical orientation, experience, intuition,
and consultation, as to which combination leads to the best working process to reach the intended goals.

Goal Setting

Aims, purposes, and objectives are included in the definition and discussion of goals. The therapist's goals and philosophical approaches are influenced by the composition and model of group therapy. Frequently reasons for referral develop into treatment goals. These are long-range, short-range or intermediate, general or specific, for the group as a whole and for the individual child. All are intimately related to the overall treatment plan for the group and the child.

Individual goals are set by the child and the therapist together. If the child has difficulty formulating his or her own, the therapist encourages and helps him or her to participate in the process. The child's parents may or may not be present during this formulation. Adolescents frequently set them alone with the therapist, whereas preschoolers have them mainly set for them by the parent and therapist in the child's presence. The goals depend on motivation and capacity to work on them.

When group composition is known, the therapist defines a tentative set of group goals; these are more formally set by the therapist and group together after the group begins. The group goals often are established from individual goals that may be common with other group members. They further need to be realistic, not too difficult, and obtainable. In addition to goal formulation, Rose (1972) and Churchill (1959) advocate setting individual and group objectives for every meeting.

Lowy (1976) states six principles relating to the goal formulation process. Goals should stem from diagnostic assessments, be stated in behavioral terms with a desired outcome, refer to improved functioning, be achievable, be ordered according to priorities, and be a shared process between members and workers (Lowy, p. 13).

The following is a sampling of possible individual and group goals:

Learn social skills (getting along with others)

Learn to trust and be open

Learn how to become a friend

Learn how you feel about peers and siblings

Learn to share

Learn to observe how others handle conflicts

Learn alternative modes of looking at and responding to situations

Learn to change patterns of relating, i.e., bully, cry baby, know-it-all, mother's helper

Learn to develop group membership and identification

Learn self-skills (who you are, what makes your self-system work)

Learn to recognize, label, and talk about feelings

Learn to talk about yourself (what you want from yourself and others)

Learn how to get feedback about your behavior and personality characteristics

Learn about your defense mechanisms

Learn how you cope and handle stress

Learn new ways to soothe and comfort self

Get help seeing and maintaining reality contact

Develop a positive social self-concept

Learn to get along with adults

Learn how you feel about adults

Learn to trust and be open with adults

Work on individual contracts and/or concrete goals

Stay in the room for 10 minutes

Refrain from physically hurting anyone

Refrain from whining or hitting

Talk instead of hitting

Stop thumb sucking

Increase discussion time from 5 to 10 minutes

Structuring and Setting Up the Group

Decisions about the group's structure are also made during stage I and must meet the needs and capacities of the children.

The authors' definition of structure differs somewhat from common usuage. It includes format and method of introducing the function, limitations, and dimensions of the therapeutic relationship. It is inherently related to the role and function of the therapist and use of group time and activities.

A common structure for latency-age groups is to divide the group's time into an activity and a discussion phase. Some hold the activity phase first (Schachter, 1974; Schiffer, 1977), whereas others hold it second (Anthony, 1973; Karson, 1965). Anthony utilizes the discussion phase to choose an activity for the group during the activity phase. Soble and Geller (1964) begin with discussion followed by activity and end with a closure phase of snacks. Frequently the verbal portion begins with 10 minutes and is gradually extended as the group's capabilities for discussion increase. Karson prefers meeting in a conference room for the talking portion and in a playroom with expressive toys for the activity time. Some therapists divide time between play and discussion flexibly. Activity group therapy (Slavson and Schiffer, 1975) and play group therapy (Ginott, 1961) are unstructured, remaining in the activity room or playroom for the entire session and not formally changing formats.

Room, equipment, and space requirements for conducting group therapy vary, depending on the model utilized and how activities are incorporated. Although typically excluded from group psychotherapy literature, social group workers have done rather detailed program analyses, matching activities to specific group requirements, taking into account age needs, space limitations, and developmental stages (Churchill, 1959; Little & Konopka, 1947; Redl & Wineman, 1957). Ganter et al. (1967) present an example of utilizing repetitive limited activities to provide necessary limits and boundaries that seriously disturbed children can incorporate, while also providing successful skills and learning experiences. Although Whittaker (1974) advocates the creative use of activities, he does so only after exploring the "built-in" dimensions of the activity and the individual and group variables. After analyzing program activities along six dimensions, he establishes an "ideal activity profile" for each child in a group (pp. 244–257). Anthony (1973) carefully structures territories and color-codes toys for each child on a small table.

Slavson and Schiffer (1975) set rather specific requirements for the room and its contents in activity group therapy (pp. 55–85). Ginott (1961) stresses the importance of room size and contents (pp. 63–78) and provides a rationale for toy selection in play group therapy (pp. 51–62). Levine (1979) states that limits should be built into the room and play materials to reduce the destructive potential and to avoid having the therapist set too many limits. Sugar (1974) focuses on content that encourages fantasy, discouraging weekly introduction of new stimuli, crafts, and destructive or hazardous materials (pp. 654–656).

When incorporating activities into the group, close consideration should be paid to matching the activities' built-in dimensions with the specific group composition and goals. These activities influence the management and process of the group, sometimes adversely. A room large enough to contain comfortably six to eight children with one or two adults is recommended. If soundproofing is not available, the room should be situated so that noise levels do not disturb adjacent personnel. It should be free from distractions while still maintaining a bright and cheerful look. Everything in the room should be childproof, and furniture should be sturdy, safe, sized for children, and washable. If not enough attention is placed on childproofing the room and the equipment prior to beginning the group, the therapist will spend much of his or her time protecting agency equipment and worrying about damage. The children should feel comfortable in the room, knowing that for the time it belongs to their group. One-way mirrors, tape recorders, or audiovisual equipment may be present; however, the therapy is for the children, and such equipment should never be used without their knowledge and permission.

Groups are either open-ended, able to add and terminate members throughout their existence, or closed, beginning and ending with essentially the same children. Setting, academic, and training needs tend to influence this structure. It is helpful to view groups as closed in principle, with the population remaining the same except for replacing dropouts.

Snacks often are utilized with varying degrees of emphasis by group therapists as part of the therapy. They are of symbolic importance both to the child and to the therapist, often being set out in a nonthreatening manner. Some groups center interaction around the snack time, with members taking a progressively more active part in their planning and disbursement. Although activity group therapy utilizes snacks throughout the group's existence, Sugar (1974) mainly offers them as a stimulus organizer in the beginning stage of the group.

Establishing a Mutual Working Agreement or Treatment Contract

Any treatment agreement must involve both therapist and patient, and in the case of children, their parents. The agreement, established during the screening interview, includes mutually shared and understood goals, obligations in accomplishing these, and expected outcome. Theoretical orientation, children's needs, and agency requirements influence whether this is informal or a formalized signed contract. Rose (1972) further differentiates between treatment and behavioral contracts (pp. 95–105).

There have been recent advocates in the field, often pressured by outside bodies responsible for evaluation and funding, who believe the more explicit the agreement, the easier it is to see and measure results. The move in this direction has challenged more traditional therapists to put their purposes and intentions into clearer, measurable goals.

The following issues are included in the agreement or contract-making process: the problems to be worked on; the desired goals; and the therapist's, child's, and parents' responsibilities. The therapist is there to prepare and help with difficulties encountered during the treatment process. He or she informs the parents that during certain periods the child's behavior might seem to worsen, that the child may feel resistant and not want to come at times. The therapist states the child's and parents' conditions of the treatment: the child is expected to come to every session on time, to stay for the whole session, and to participate; the parents are expected to assure the child's attendance, canceling only for good reasons, to communicate if developments arise that may affect the child, to adjust to temporary and long-term changes in behavior as outlined and planned for, and to engage in whatever treatment process has been recommended for themselves. The younger or more disturbed the child is, the greater is the parental responsibility. Adolescents may take considerable responsibility for arranging their treatment, including making the initial contact with the therapist. Contract making and signing are frequently utilized with adolescents and help to eliminate their use of denial and projection. When financial arrangements are a part of the therapist's role definition, they are included at this point.

Croxton (1974) views contract setting as a gradual and complex sequence following these phases; exploratory, negotiation, preliminary contract, working agreement, secondary contracts among group members, termination, and evaluation.

Throughout this process the therapist helps the parents and child identify, verbalize, and deal with some of the unresolved feelings they may have regarding their participation in the treatment process. The degree of formality in the sealing of this agreement may vary from an affirmative nod, handshake, or verbalized statement to a written and signed document. Once "sealed," it enables the therapist, the child, and the parents to proceed. They agree on the date and time of the first group meeting.

Length of Sessions, Duration of Group

Once setting, philosophy, therapeutic goals, and age are established, the length of sessions and duration of the group fall naturally into place. As a rule of thumb, the more verbal, discussion-oriented the group, the less time it can tolerate, unless it's very intact. Generally, groups can handle 45 minutes. Groups having both activity and discussion periods can be at least 60 minutes in length with 30 minute periods or 20- to 40-minute periods. Gradually, the talking time can be increased to 30 to 40 minutes as the group progresses through the year. A highly anxious group may be able to begin with only 10 minutes of discussion. Sugar (1974) feels that outpatient preschool and early latency-age groups can handle 45 to 60 minutes weekly of interpretive therapy.

Play and activity groups often can handle longer periods of time. Slavson's activity group therapy requires 1½ hours weekly for several years. His activity-interview groups meet weekly for 90 minutes to 2 hours.

Forty-five minutes often works well for latency-age and young adolescents, while 60 to 90 minutes may be very appropriate for older adolescents. Levine (1979) theorizes that "much of the flagrant behavior reported in groups of latency-aged school children stems from the threat of too long a meeting" and that as much as 30 to 40 minutes of this behavior is largely to fend off threatening discussions or experiences (p. 21). Fifteen minutes two to three times a week may be a good format.

Duration of groups also relates to setting, philosophy, and staffing needs. Some settings follow children's school schedules or trainees' schedules, which may last 6 to 9 months or 1 to 2 years. Longer-term psychoanalytic groups frequently meet 1½ to 2 years. Some open-ended groups go on rather indefinitely. Short-term groups generally run from 3 to 6 months, and diagnostic groups four sessions.

References

Anthony, E. J. (1973). Group-analytic psychotherapy with children and adolescents. In S. H. Foulkes & E. J. Anthony *Group Psychotherapy: The psychoanalytic approach* (rev. 2nd ed.). Baltimore: Penguin Books. pp. 186–232.

Axline, M. (1947). *Play therapy*. Boston: Houghton Mifflin.

Barcai, A., & Robinson, E. H. (1969). Conventional group therapy with preadolescent children. *International Journal of Group Psychotherapy, 19*, 334–345.

Bertcher, H. J., & Maple, F. (1974). Elements and issues in group composition. In R. Glasser, R. Sarri, & R. Vinter (Eds.), *Individual change through small groups*. New York: Free Press. pp. 186–208.

Braaten, L. E. (1974/1975). Developmental phases of encounter groups and related intensive groups. *Interpersonal Development, 5*, 112–129.

Charach, R. (1983). Brief interpretive group psychotherapy with early latency-age children. *International Journal of Group Psychotherapy, 33*, 349–364.

Churchill, S. R. (1959). Prestructuring group content. *Social Work, 4*, 52–59.

Churchill, S. R. (1965). Social group work: A diagnostic tool in child guidance. *American Journal of Orthopsychiatry, 35*, 581–588.

Croxton, T. A. (1974). The therapeutic contract in social treatment. In P. Glasser, R. Sarri, & R. Vinter (Eds.), *Individual change through small groups.* New York: Free Press. pp. 168–185.

Demsch, B., & Brekelbaum, B. (1969). Exceptionality-change through the group. *Journal of Pupil Personnel Workers, 13*, 137–141.

Frank, M. G. (1976). Modifications of activity group therapy: Responses to ego-impoverished children. *Clinical Social Work Journal, 4*, 102–109.

Ganter, G., & Polansky, N. A. (1964). Predicting a child's accessibility to individual treatment from diagnostic groups. *Social Work, 9*, 56–63.

Ganter, G., Yeakel, M., & Polansky, N. A. (1967). *Retrieval from limbo: The intermediary group treatment of inaccessible children.* New York: Child Welfare League.

Ginott, H. G. (1961). *Group psychotherapy with children.* New York: McGraw-Hill.

Gratton, L., & Pope, L. (1972). Group diagnosis and therapy for young school children. *Hospital and Community Psychiatry, 23*, 180–200.

Johnson, D. L., & Gold, S. R. (1971). An empirical approach to issues of selection and evaluation in group therapy. *International Journal of Group Psychotherapy, 21*, 321–339.

Kadis, A. L., Krasner, J. D., Winick, C., & Foulkes, S. H. (1963). *A practicum of group psychotherapy.* New York: Harper & Row.

Karson, S. (1965). Group psychotherapy with latency age boys. *International Journal of Group Psychotherapy, 15*, 81–89.

Levine, B. (1979). *Group psychotherapy practice and development,* Englewood Cliffs, NJ: Prentice-Hall.

Lifton, N., & Smolen, E. M. (1966). Group psychotherapy with schizophrenic children. *International Journal of Group Psychotherapy, 16*, 23–41.

Little, H. M., & Konopka, G. (1947). Group therapy in a child guidance center. *American Journal of Orthopsychiatry, 17*, 303–311.

Lowy, L. (1976). Goal formulation in social work with groups. In S. Bernstein (Ed.), *Further explorations in group work.* Boston: Charles River Books. pp. 116–144.

Paradise, R., & Daniels, R. (1976). Group composition as a treatment tool with children. In S. Bernstein (Ed.), *Further explorations in group work.* Boston: Charles River Books. pp. 34–35.

Peck, M. L., & Stewart, R. H. (1964). Current practices in selection criteria for group play-therapy. *Journal of Clinical Psychology, 20*, 146.

Redl, F. (1944). Diagnostic group work. *American Journal of Orthopsychiatry, 14*, 53–67.

Redl, F., & Wineman, D. (1957). *The aggressive child.* New York: Free Press.

Rose, S. D. (1972). *Treating children in groups: A behavioral approach.* San Francisco: Jossey-Bass.

Sarri, R. C., & Galinsky, M. J. (1974). A conceptual framework for group development. In P. Glasser, R. Sarri, & R. Vinter (Eds.), *Individual change through small groups.* New York: Free Press. pp. 71–88.

Schachter, R. S. (1974). Kinetic psychotherapy in the treatment of children. *American Journal of Psychotherapy, 28*, 430–437.

Scheidlinger, S. (1960). Experimental group treatment of severely deprived latency age children. *American Journal of Orthopsychiatry, 30*, 356–368.

Scheidlinger, S. (1965). Three approaches with socially deprived latency age children. *International Journal of Group Psychotherapy, 15*, 434–445.

Schiffer, M. (1969). *Therapeutic play group.* New York: Grune & Stratton.

Schiffer, M. (1977). Activity-interview group psychotherapy: Theory, principles, and practice. *International Journal of Group Psychotherapy, 27*, 377–388.

Slavson, S. R. (1955). Criteria for selection and rejection of patients for various types of group psychotherapy. *International Journal of Group Psychotherapy, 5*, 3–30.

Slavson, S. R., & Schiffer, M. (1975). *Group psychotherapies for children.* New York: International Universities Press.

Soble, D., & Geller, J. J. (1964). A type of group psychotherapy in the children's unit of a mental hospital. *Psychiatric Quarterly, 38*, 262–270.

Speers, R. W., & Lansing, C. (1965). *Group therapy in childhood psychoses.* Chapel Hill, NC: University of North Carolina Press.

Sugar, M. (1974). Interpretive group psychotherapy with latency children. *Journal of the American Academy of Child Psychiatry, 13*, 648–666.

Whitaker, D. S., & Lieberman, M. A. (1964). *Psychotherapy through group process.* New York: Atherton Press.

Whittaker, J. K. (1974). Program activities: Their selection and use in a therapeutic milieu. In P. Glasser, R. Sarri, & R. Vinter (Eds.), *Individual change through small groups*. New York: Free Press. pp. 244–257.

Yalom, I. D. (1970). *The theory and practice of group psychotherapy*. New York: Basic Books.

Chapter 4

STAGE II: EXPLORATION

Anita K. Lampel

EXPERIENTIAL DESCRIPTION

"Am I supposed to wait here? Who's going to come and get me?" While one child looks sullenly or despondently at his shoes, another nervously paces. Some try to guess who is in the group. The children look at each other, as if at a birthday party for someone they don't know. They wait.

Then the therapist comes. His arrival decreases the anxiety of children and parents, while others wonder if "he'll forget I'm here." As feelings run through the children's minds, they focus on the therapist. Almost inevitably, they are on their best behavior as they walk toward the therapy room. Two jostle for a place beside the therapist; it seems safer there.

"So this is the therapy room. What's in here? Is it okay to look?" The children peel off each other and the therapist. One tentatively explores the room, wondering what the therapist will say. Another looks at the other children, hoping for a confirmation that this is in fact a place where other children are like him and where he can find a friend.

The birthday party feeling lingers for a while. Children

look gay, exchange pleasantries and names. After all, no one's mother is here, and the kids don't seem so bad after all. A quiet hum settles over the room. There are signs that this is not like anything the child has known before. The children look at each other again, but differently. Almost visible is the assessment each child makes. Then they look back to the therapist for more structure and understanding of the difference they are beginning to feel.

One child tentatively reexplores the room, wondering if he will touch some forbidden object; another hovers near the therapist; still another attempts to be "mother's little helper"; while another ignores the therapist in favor of his peers. As they interact with each other, verbal and nonverbal questions are directed to the therapist, often disguised in behavior. Underneath, the child wonders, "If I'm good maybe I can go," "If I'm good maybe I can stay," or just "If . . . " The the therapist moves in with quiet verbal and nonverbal answers to the unspoken questions. Some therapists do this with structure, formally stating the goals, limits, and expectations. Others wait for questions or for the situations to arise before introducing these. Still others may step back but actively initiate responses from the children about why they are here and what they would like to do in the group and get from it.

The room and children may be fairly calm for several sessions. This period may be a honeymoon, as the children gather their resources to cope with the newness of the experience and the anticipation of what is to come. Colleagues who have run groups before discover that the novice therapist is in their offices more than previously. "Hey, this isn't nearly as bad as you said it was going to be" reflects the therapist's genial interest in his group's psychodynamics at this point. For those who have done groups before or who find the concept exciting, much discussion is generated.

Suddenly, the quasi-group feeling disappears and discrete individuals reappear, each moving emotionally and behaviorally. Each child is caught up in this first expression of heightened anxiety. "Maybe this is something I'm not supposed to do." "Let me try it." "Boy, I'm going to get that kid." "I'm just going to sit here under the table." "I'm going to make this place just like every other place I've known." These messages buzz around on a nonverbal level. The behaviors push and pull at the children and the therapist. "What is he going to do?" "What isn't he going to do?" "How different is this place really?" "Can he take it?"

For some children it is as if their senses are now more acute, almost embattled. Others, also anxious, are almost unaware of what is transpiring, observing everything through a dense fog. For one or two, anxiety arises around the exploration of limits. For still others it is the mere formalization of the group and the presence of the other children that precipitates the anxiety. In one or two children the anxiety rises quickly to a level where it must be expressed. It's catch as catch can for the therapist as he hurriedly moves in to express something to one child, only to have another begin to do or say something that also requires therapeutic intervention.

Then Chris begins to miss sessions. The therapist calls to find out why. Mom says, "Well, Chris just didn't want to go and I didn't feel I could make him," or "Baseball practice is on that day," or "He's worse since he's started," or "I don't know . . ." A 5-minute phone call easily stretches to 30 minutes while the therapist attempts to help the parents reassess what Chris's need for therapy is, what Chris might or might not be trying to get out of refusing to come, and what is going on in the parents' lives that might be influencing the refusal. The therapist begins to realize this is not easily straightened out over the telephone and decides to talk to the parents' group therapist or have the parents come in to see him. What is the best way to proceed in helping? The therapist experiences anger and a drain on his time and energy. He has struggled to get the group together, and already it's being disrupted. If this child does not return to the group, he becomes the first dropout. As the therapist moves to handle the necessary arrangements, he feels pain and a hurt ego.

Sometimes, even this early, the therapist and consultant realize a mistake has been made in the selection of a child. Brad is tearing the room apart despite all controls. The other children are afraid of him and don't want to come back. The therapist grows increasingly uncomfortable with his behavior with the other children, fearing for their safety. When the therapist determines Brad isn't right and that the children can handle his being dropped better than they can his continued presence, he experiences a sense of relief. The therapis   lls the parents in for an interview. Sometimes parents hear t'   statement with relief; others react angrily to the implication that their child cannot make it and reject any further overtures.

Reparative work is necessary within the group to help them understand why Brad had been removed. The therapist repeats reassuringly, "We will help Brad but in another way. I am not angry at him. We will help all of you in the way it seems best for you." Even with this offered reassurance, the therapist notes a sudden, even more acute rise in anxiety. Those children in the group for whom the group is beginning to work become conspicuous by their behavior after the removal is announced. They are fearful that they too may lose that which is gaining in increased importance. Such children require reassurance at a more sophisticated level than those who accept the disappearance with equanimity. To some children the group has not yet gained such importance.

Some children have caught on to what is supposed to happen. One child brings the events of the day into therapy. Another mentions he had a fight with his brother. Often his nascent comments are lost or ignored by the others but are treasured by the therapist. Another seems to have ceased a particular mode of reacting to others, and the therapist can see trust in himself and the group deepening. Still another, though, seems caught in the earliest sessions of the group, unable or unwilling to move with the others. The child repetitiously resists, acts out, or withdraws. The therapist persistently repeats messages of acceptance, understanding, and patience, educating that this group is different from outside experiences and relationships. The child still comes and the therapist hopes that as the group progresses, this child, even though moving slower than the rest, will nonetheless make progress in allowing these needed trusting relationships with himself and the group to develop.

Outside the group therapy sessions, some changes are beginning to occur. Parents and school may be noting a change in the child's behavior. There may be less acting out at school or less negativism at home, often a sign that the child's conflict is beginning to be brought to and contained within the therapy group. Occasionally, a parent will note that their child appears angrier or sadder than usual.

The changes are seen too in the waiting room. Johnny, whose maniacal behavior in the group declared all to be his enemy, seeks out the company of Bobby as he arrives. Together, they peer anxiously out to see whoever is going to come. The next child may be greeted with catcalls, derision, or fisticuffs, in recognition of the child's status within the group as a sign that the group is forming. The therapist arrives to find all of the children in the group interacting in the waiting room. His arrival acts as a catalyst and focal point for communication within the group, as an expectant air settles over the ongoing communication, no matter how wild it may be. Each child expects that the therapist will be there, will do or say something, and that there is safety in what happens.

Within the group, the key for the child is "Where is *my* place?" Each child throws himself at the therapist and at the other children. Even the one who withdraws, seeming to ask for no place at all, is testing whether that place will be allowed him or if the therapist and the group will chase him out. Much of the activity seems to have little to do with limit testing but rather with: "Can you see me? Can you hear me? Is it okay if I stay here? Where do I fit in?" The search for alliances with the therapist and individual members of the group is more obvious now. Some children react with delight to one another, behaving in perfectly appropriate ways. An alliance that disappeared within 10 minutes now lasts for 30. Occasionally an immediate twosome will form.

Reacting to the activity and anxiety surrounding the search for a place in the group, the therapist increases the number of reassuring and including remarks. "I know you are here. I care about each of you. You are important to me." When each child finds his place, no matter how low in status in the group that place may be, some of the anxiety will diminish. A pecking order or status and role emerges in which each child seems, for a time, to be satisfied.

The therapist feels, from time to time, like a ghost in the machine. His words can scarcely be heard above the din of each child's active involvement with the others. But through it all the child asks, "Where is my place with *you*?" The therapist answers verbally, "It is here with *me and the group*. He cannot show favoritism for one, focus only on individual issues or only on group issues. He is shared and has apparent concern for all. His comments to one must be heard as a comment to all. "You can trust me." "I do understand." "It is hard." "It's okay to feel that way, but not always to act that way." "Feelings can be talked about, shared, and understood." The therapist finds himself moving from child to child, subgroup to subgroup, communicating to individuals yet introducing the "we" essential to group development. "Does anyone else feel that way?" "Has that ever happened to you?" "Do you understand what Mark is trying to say?" The therapist experiences himself as both inside and outside of the group. Outside because he cannot be a part of the pecking order, inside because it is from here that he is accepted and must establish a safe, therapeutic climate. Trust in the therapist must be marshaled against the testing to come.

One by one the children begin to hear and believe that the therapist is there for one and for all. Anxiety diminishes if only by just-noticeable degrees. The fact of the group and the therapist's presence takes on importance in the child's life. Mother reports that Johnny was upset when the teacher kept him after school.

The children begin labeling the group, one by one, at home, school, and in the waiting room. "I am here for *my* group," one says to the receptionist. "Where are the kids in *my* group?" another says. "In *my group* . . ."

DYNAMIC DESCRIPTION

The *exploration stage* begins with the first session and ends as individuals in the group have invested enough in the group to personalize and label it as "*my* group." This may last anywhere from several sessions up to several months, partially depending on how reserved the group tends to be and whether the group is long-term. Groups of severely disturbed children may have as their ultimate group goal merely to complete this stage.

Stage II can be divided into three phases for illustration of development and progression of individual and group processes. In the first phase the children check out various hypotheses about the therapist and the other children. These represent the growth of initial trust in the therapist and the group, enough to bring them back to a second and third session. The children who pass through this phase are able to tolerate a therapeutic environment, a therapist, and a group of peers who do not conform entirely to expectations. The ability to tolerate this rests primarily on the child's pathology and strength at this point. The therapist uses his or her clinical skills to help the children hear the message they need to hear: "You are all right here."

In the second phase, the children more actively test the therapist's tolerance for mildly disruptive behavior. In this instance the children seem to be asking, "Can you handle this minimal indication of what I'm really like?" The minor infractions of limits and house rules may seem like major infractions to the novice therapist. The key is that these are carried out in an air of expectancy by the children. Again, the primary message on which the therapist must concentrate is, "Yes, I see that and still care about you. Yes, I can handle that."

Finally, the children are ready to accept the therapist and the presence of the other children. They are not yet ready to accept the group as a vehicle of behavioral and emotional change even though such changes already may have occurred. They are, however, ready to accept the therapist as a trustworthy person, as a person who can accept and deal with some of the behavior that has been troublesome to them in the past. It may be assumed that the other children exist, for the most part, as the setting in which each child and the therapist must form their private bond of trust. This achieved step, the labeling identity of the group, signals the end of Stage II: the child's acceptance of his or her place with the therapist, among the other children,

Other authors have formulated an opening stage of group psychotherapy with children (Rose, 1972; Sarri & Galinsky, 1974; Sugar, 1974) and adolescents (Bracklemanns & Berkovitz,

1972). Bracklemanns and Berkovitz earmark this opening stage the "Fragmented Stage," with the group operating "in a very chaotic, disjointed and disruptive fashion" (p. 43). In a separate article Berkovitz (1972) states that during the first four or five sessions the status roles may be in the process of formation. Slavson and Schiffer (1975) report that the children initially experience a "shock effect" and relate primarily to the activities available and secondarily and minimally to the other persons.

Rose (1972) outlines techniques for the initial phase to enable the children to move into the therapy and to maintain attention and attendance. Similarly, other behaviorally oriented therapists address the issues of contract setting and reinforcement of appropriate behavior beginning with the initial setting. They seldom address early relationships among group members or between members and the therapist, except as defined contractually, such as contracting for taking turns during discussion.

Sugar (1974) isolates three phenomena that characterize the initial phase: The children "are learning to get along in the group"; the child shows initial resistance "related to his realistic disappointment in the anticipated functioning of the therapist in the frustration of his transference expectations"; "there are also the frequent, intense dependency needs" (p. 656).

More variation is seen regarding the criteria for the ending of this first stage. Bracklemanns and Berkovitz (1972) state that the ending of the "preworking stage" is heralded by a commitment of the members to each other and a "unit-ness" of the group. Sugar (1974) feels the end of the initial phase is signaled by "a certain amount of relative stability in the group dynamics and only relative cohesion" (p. 656).

The Child

The children and the therapist are anxious about the first group session. "This anxiety ensures the success of the first meeting since, after being together for a short while, everyone discovers that his fears were unjustified. The relief from the anticipatory anxiety is a great morale raiser" (Sugar, 1974, p. 656).

First, there is "Who am I here?" The child's expectations and hopes for the group help to determine what aspects of the information available about the group characteristics are assessed. Anxiety level also is a determining factor in the initial analysis of data. The more anxious child gathers reality data more slowly than the less anxious child.

Then, "Who are you?" The only person the child knows and has had interpersonal contact with is the therapist. The therapist becomes the buffer for anxiety. The child reacts to the therapist according to the child's dynamics, his or her ability to trust, and whatever relationship he or she developed with the therapist during stage I. The child indicates, "Let's you and me . . ." to the therapist; only to be answered, "Let's you, me and . . ."

Then the children move into a more active phase determining the boundaries of the room, therapist, and peers. Each child reacts characterologically in a manner that is functional and typical of him or her. Although the pattern has pathological elements, the child struggles here in stage II to keep these in check. Whatever ego strengths he or she possesses are used to maintain the balance between the emotional and environmental press.

Each child experiences transference, which becomes confused with the reality of the therapist and the therapeutic climate. Relief may be felt by one child who feared the therapist would be like his or her angry mother or teacher. Another child, though, with similar history, finds the therapist's approaches frightening and fights to maintain status quo. The environment is different. The permission to express emotional tensions is different. The balance within the child begins to shift.

During phase one, the child begins to form and test various hypotheses. Predetermined fantasy and expectations begin to confront reality as the child sees it. Even such simple items as the room, time, and structure of the group repeated ad nauseam help to reduce the children's anxieties. They experience stability, predictability, and support from therapist in testing their hypotheses.

As anxieties over forming new hypotheses drop, anxieties over testing them rise, sometimes precipitously, and the group enters phase two. The child is propelled to reveal more pathology, which asks of the therapist, "Can you handle this beginning revelation of my innermost being?" The upsurge in anxiety appears to be related to the rigidity of the child's defenses and pressure of perceived unacceptable feelings and behavior. The therapist's response, "I see what you are showing me and I can handle it and I still care about you," contributes to change. A change of hypotheses means that new information has been processed by the child. Each child is in the process of assessing whether and how the group can function for him or her.

By now the children are beginning to look quite disturbed. The movement has been from tentative exploration of environment to the exploration of limits. From time to time a subgroup is formed, but these alliances break off and each child again operates on his or her own. Another dyad forms and may indicate pathological needs are partially met by this friendship.

The dropout and absenteeism rates can be high during this stage. For one, there is the child who cannot explore at the same pace as the others. Perhaps his reality checking is too poor, his anxiety too high, his inhibitions too great, or his defenses too rigid. He is left behind as the others stabilize their personal environment. One child may by expression, posture, and verbalization show this is not really what he wanted or bargained for, and quickly reneges on his therapeutic contract. Another, finds he "hates" the therapist for his size, sex, or something. This is a strong initial negative transference, and the therapist may not have time within the group to help the child work it through. The child, therefore, is unable to depend on or use the therapist as an anxiety buffer. On occasion this child can be maintained through this stage because of his strong alliance with another group member, such as in a dyad.

There is also the child who feels he is hated by the others. He is likely to be the one referred to as "always picked on" or the "school bully." He operates so quickly to confirm his hypotheses that the therapist, try as he may, has not seen how the child sets it up. This child may decide he is once again being scapegoated and will leave, or he may linger long enough for the therapist to see the setup and intervene.

Removing a child is painful for both the child and therapist. Some children are angry and defensive, experiencing rejection once again. Some are sad and are able to express their hurt. Still others feel relief because they too were aware that this group or group psychotherapy did not feel right.

By now the fact that Johnny is here means that Mark will do or say certain things to Johnny. That Melissa is here will mean that Elizabeth will seek her out and that they will huddle together. One child seems to make things happen, always his or her own way. Even changes in dress, in physical appearance, come to mean certain things to each child, the group, and the therapist. Within the group, the child is determining the strengths and weaknesses of the others. Each child has placed others in roles he or she finds most comfortable and has found the most comfortable niche for himself or herself. These roles are most likely superficial, carry-overs from the past.

Throughout the group's short existence, each child leaves the group after each session having had at least one question answered. Under these is the unspoken one, "Can I trust enough to come back again?" The child looks for reasons to come back, and the therapist supports these; the child looks for reasons not to and the therapist works to mitigate those reasons. The exploration is at an experiential level and the ground grows firmer.

The therapeutic work for the children began on day 1. By the end of stage II, they have accomplished a measurable amount. They have assessed the therapeutic situation as different from other situations. They have shown the therapist and the other children something of who they feel they really are, a preliminary statement to be worked on for the remainder of group therapy. They have begun to trust the therapist and through this are beginning to hear the therapeutic communication and respond accordingly.

The Therapist

Therapeutic assessment, too, begins on day 1. The children are in a new environment, a mode of therapy chosen because it is most appropriate for them. The therapist listens, observes, and hypothesizes on similar questions about each child. Does the child isolate himself or move toward others? Does he attach himself in a symbiotic way or can he be independent? Does he accept or reject overtures from peers and therapist? What is appropriate or inappropriate about his behavior? Is he provocative or is he withdrawn?

Things run very smoothly during the first phase, so it often appears to the therapist that he or she has chosen a normally reacting group of children. This initial positive transference is experienced because the therapist is seen as the only source of expectation, authority, and gratification in the group, a relationship begun during the preparation stage. The child's dependency needs and disappointment at unmet gratification of needs are less intense during this stage than during the other stages of group therapy. During this phase the novice therapist may experience relief that group therapy does not seem too difficult or demand too much; bewilderment due to feeling unsure about what is occurring and whether he or she should attempt to do anything about it; overwhelmed by the awesome responsibility of relating to so many needs of so many children at one time.

As the anxiety begins to rise, the therapist reconvinces himself or herself that the children are disturbed. The novice therapist is beginning to appreciate difficulties surrounding group therapy with children. If the therapist has an eye for subtle flashes of dynamics, he or she begins to store these up. He or she continues making assessments of what the group may do for each child; and may also feel that he or she is gradually being torn asunder by the effort to draw all the children, each tugging away, into the semblance of a group. Some therapists can relax a little in these opening phases, while others wonder how a group will ever be formed of these vying individuals.

By now, the therapist has begun assessing underpinnings of behavior, noticing a quick change of subject or appearance of inappropriate behavior as the result of the theme being expressed. The therapist notes the child who approaches each situation stereotypically. He or she has caught flashes of deep anger directed against other children or against the therapist. He or she notes the child who pushes limits consistently. The therapist makes note of a dyad forming and watches its development, knowing that this can be destructive for a group and may need to be split up. Or provided the dyad can gradually allow others to share in its intimacy, it may facilitate group cohesion. The therapist functions much as a "radar system" (Berkovitz) as he or she scans the scene looking for scenarios, assessing them for plot, motive, and affective valence.

Next, the therapist works on formulating some plans for individualizing therapy; trying to match technique with behavior to facilitate solidifying the initial treatment contract. Sometimes these contracts have to be reassessed and negotiated. As he or she begins to intervene therapeutically, the therapist realizes he or she has begun that which is so unique and powerful in group therapy: to conduct therapy during the actual behavioral crisis rather than after it. Outside the group the therapist spends considerable time with a consultant, assessing children and treatment techniques. Inside the group the therapist is seen setting limits, communicating support, educating, and clarifying.

As the children pass into phase three the therapist realizes that the child is asking something special of him or her. The therapist continues to work hard at the message of trust, strength, and inclusion. "You do have a place with me and with the group." Sensitized to the children who are forming a bond of trust with him or her, the therapist cements this and anticipates using this nucleus to draw the others in. It is a judicious blend of movement toward peers and movement toward himself or herself that the therapist tries to obtain. Moving from child to child, subgroup to subgroup, the therapist communicates to individuals yet uses the essential "we" in the attempt to get the children to relate to each other and to the concept of a group. The therapist gradually expands the dependence on himself or herself to dependence on the group, eventually to open avenues of communication and interdependence with the group members.

The Group

It is day 1. The group is more an administrative definition than a group. Group formation and development is just beginning, as is the therapy within it. By the end of stage II the group is embryonic. The children have jostled to find a place with the other children. They have come to recognize that the other children will be there with them. Acceptance of peers within the therapy time and space and the formation of brief subgroups for many purposes is the initial stage of group formation around the central figure of the therapist. A birthday party is not a group for therapy, nor are the individually anxious children, nor are children cemented only to the therapist. But as the children interact with one another, use one another, like and dislike one another, group formation has begun. The therapist has begun the messages of "we-ness," but the group has a long way to go before it is cohesive.

The Parents

Many parents are optimistic about the course of therapy and engage willingly in sessions around their child's behavior. They are often curious about their child's therapy group and can be aided to turn this energy to working on issues within the home. Some parents have concern about the "excitement" or "wildness" they observe in the waiting room before or after the group session and worry that their children are getting over-stimulated. Others have an emotional state paralleling their child's. "What are you doing to my kid?" The message comes across to the therapist, who may react with a sudden, brief flash of anger. The therapist feels pulled into the family dynamics again despite the fact that the contractual arrangement and need for therapy had been clearly understood by all parties.

Some parents may feel the need to collude with the child as the child begins to push to be absent or to drop the group. They begin to realize what the contract really means in terms of time and effort. They are unsure, regretting their commitment, involvement, and the pressure they exerted to get the child in the group. Some may have a negative transference, partially due to a buildup of resentments against authority and the agencies who have previously dealt with their child. Even the firmest of contractual agreements does not guard totally against family pathology. Reaffirming or solidifying the therapeutic contractual agreement requires more frequent contact with the parents. The therapist may find himself or herself engaged in direct work with the parents.

Disorganized families, families with a very disturbed parent, and families without socioeconomic resources, sometimes drop out from therapy. It is during this stage or stage III that this most frequently occurs.

The Agency

During consultation certain patterns begin to emerge. The therapist arrives with a predominant emotion, usually carried over from the group. A blow-by-blow account of the group or a focus on particular interactions reveals the generator for the feelings. Emerging roles and patterns of behavior are followed closely. A discussion of the possible dynamics of the relationship, child or status of the group leads into possible next steps for the therapist. In addition to focusing on beginning therapeutic communication, the therapist is shown how to foster beginning group development.

The agency is being called on to share with the therapist. Potentially good therapists may be turned from the use of group therapy at this point, not by the group experience, which is going well, but by the isolation from other therapists or the agency during the early group therapy sessions.

The agency plays its most important role during stage II with regard to "house rules." In house rules rest the needs of the agency to protect the physical plant and to keep operations running smoothly. The agency's secondary role is providing back-up and alternative resources for children who drop or are dropped from groups.

SPECIAL ISSUES

Structured or Unstructured Groups

The therapist has considered his philosophy of group treatment prior to the beginning of stage II. The therapist's chosen theory fits closest to his or her own focus and training. Theories comment on the opening phase, usually offering guidelines for structuring the first sessions. These opening sessions are used to establish the tenor of the remaining therapeutic interactions and interventions and the nature of the use of games or activities.

Groups fall along a continuum of structured to unstructured. In a structured group, the therapist begins in a limit-setting manner to direct interactions between all group members. An obvious method of doing this is to present to the children a contract for behavior during the group that specifies the expected, approved, and disapproved interactions. In some groups of older children, the first few sessions can be devoted to a discussion of their own ideas for the group's contract. The contingencies of behavior are then considered. In some groups, a point system is exchanged for privileges; in others, a point system is valued for its competitive nature.

Sometimes activities and games are utilized to force an external structure on the group's interactions. This technique is used frequently with children who do not have sufficient ego development, strength, and control to function other than in a disintegrated, fragmented, or overly aggressive manner in an open, unstructured group setting. Some severely disturbed children need the help provided by simple structured games to learn interactional skills.

Schacter (1974, 1984) utilizes specifically structured yet noncompetitive games to facilitate social interaction and mobilize feelings. "Stop the action" is a command issued when the child responds in a game with his characteristic and pathological response to a feeling such as anger. Because intervention occurs at the moment the emotion is experienced, new alternatives can be taught. Clifford and Cross (1980) describe utilizing a "Stop and Go Rule" that gives group members, in addition to the therapist, the power to prevent and control unacceptable behavior.

Ganter, Yeakel and Polansky (1967) developed very structured "standard operating procedures" for working with severely disturbed children lacking in "organizational unity" and "capacity for self-observation" (pp. 49–54). They established a strict, repetitive schedule of routine activities that progressed from simple to more organized within the activities themselves, within the session, and from session to session.

The advantages of a highly structured system are that the children are quickly led to an identification of the issues to be worked on, in terms they can grasp and manipulate verbally. Limits of behavior within the group and the applicability of such limits to behavior outside the group are labeled, and realistic contingencies are established. The therapist identifies himself, and the adult population, as "in charge of contingencies." The children's anxieties are diminished because what is expected and what will happen is immediately clarified. Disadvantages are that children are placed in the same relationship to authority that they encounter in other situations. Children are possibly implicitly informed that it is the behavior and not the emotion that is important. Relationships are initially controlled by material considerations and contingencies, and not through more natural consequences arising from the relationships and behavior.

Some therapists carefully plan activities, rather than allowing individual or group choice; others allow group decision-making. More individually oriented activities are planned during this initial stage, with gradual movement toward group orientation. Activities are planned with therapeutic goals to enhance esteem through completion, sharing of materials, and group cooperation. Churchill (1959) describes planning based on analysis of each child's group roles, happenings in the previous group session, and anticipation of issues to arise during the following session. Programming for ego support (Redl & Wineman, 1957) is utilized to try to eliminate anything "harmful to any child," although it may not be equally helpful to each member. Activites are selected as needed for diagnostic usefulness or for specific individual or group interaction.

Activity group therapy (Slavson and Schiffer, 1975) is an unstructured group, with freedom of choice of available materials and activities and no listing of rules and limits. The children's behavior is not dictated by the therapist. The therapist is a low-key, nonintrusive, accepting participant-observer. Activity group therapy is on the extreme end of the continuum with other psychoanalytically oriented therapy models operating within the unstructured range. In these groups the therapist steps back from direction of the flow of the individual and group process. He or she may then support or reinforce children who appear to be taking appropriate steps toward interaction. The therapist encourages symbolic play and revelation of conflictual material which he or she then clarifies and interprets.

The advantages of such a system are that the children are not forced to related in any particular manner, other than that which is characterologically appropriate at the time. The children are introduced to the therapist as a nondemanding adult who offers support but does not limit behavior and does not punish. The therapist imparts to the children, through support, a sense that their behavior is reasonable and understandable and that their feelings are likewise reasonable. For the therapist, such a group provides an opportunity to allow relationships and individual behaviors to occur naturally rather than through the imposition of external limitations and contingencies. Disadvantages accrue in this model also. Lack of structure can immediately increase the anxiety and decrease the intactness of aggressive, delinquent, or ego-deficient children, and of very disturbed children whose abilities to interact with others and sustain group movement are not well developed. This type of group is sometimes painfully reminiscent of a child's own life situation, perhaps a highly disorganized, undifferentiated family, and offers, at least initially, less benefit than a more structured group with its closer resemblance to reality contingencies. These children need external boundaries and expectations in relationships that provide needed ego and object supports. This approach works best in groups of several years' duration.

In homogeneous groupings of aggressive and severely acting-out children, when activities are not able completely to channel and control their impulses, the therapist must intervene and provide appropriate channeling of expression. He or she instructs, "We talk, not hit." As necessary, the therapist isolates, places a hand on the shoulder, or temporarily removes a child to the hall or a quiet room. Only if absolutely necessary does the therapist restrain the child, preferably after removal from the room.

Activities and structuring are utilized during this intial stage to help establish a beginning "groupness" and limit anxiety. As part of this structuring, a therapist may wish to introduce certain issues for discussion, and/or may allow issues to introduce themselves from the activities.

Communication Within the Group

The initial task for the therapst is to open lines of communication and to establish the expectation that communication and relationships in the group can be shared by all. The novice group therapist discovers that these aspects of language differ subtly from those found in individual therapy. At the most obvious level, group therapy involves a myriad of channels: between child and child, between therapist and child, between therapist and co-therapist, among therapist and two children, ad infinitum. What channels are open and between whom they are open, never mind what is being transacted along the channels, may be obscured or hidden in an active group of children. In addition, the therapist feels "on stage," as his or her voice is raised and nonverbal gestures are mildly exaggerated to catch and hold the attention of the group. Communication may be simplified and directed below the level the therapist would use if he or she were doing individual therapy. The "age level" of communication needs to cushion, not challenge, the abilities of the least able group member.

Clarification, or identification, is a flexible tool that can be used to draw in other members of the group. For example, the therapist may state, "I feel you are angry at Mark. Does anyone else feel that Mark is angry? How does he show it to you?" Children of a variety of ages and pathology can respond to the type of message that clarifies and labels the behavioral components of the emotional state. It can have both an educational and a group development purpose. For younger children, therapists may use doll or puppet play to illustrate this type of communication. The children's replies are then used to help the others focus on similar feelings in their own lives.

Support comments from the therapist often are directed toward a particular child for a specific behavior. "I know it's hard for you to show me that." "You are really making progress in being able to do that." "You guys are sure beginning to learn how to share." "That's great that we all came and were able to participate." This type of communication is usually quite easy for the novice therapist to provide. Nonverbal communication to the child and group must be visibly explicit.

Control, on the other hand, is a difficult communication to handle. To help the child establish his or her own controls, the therapist gives a message that the child is okay, but the behavior is not because it is unacceptable. Restrictions that are appropriate and not punitive will be placed on the child to prevent the occurrence or recurrence of the behavior. The procedures utilized will become the prototype and will establish an expectation for the group that unacceptable behaviors will be handled in a specific manner. The therapist must be prepared and equipped to handle in a therapeutic fashion all behaviors that occur. Clarification is not always easily attained, because a group agitator, sending messages of anxiety or anger, may in fact look as if he is behaving appropriately while another child acts out for him.

Interpretive comments in stage II may be minimal, depending on the material presented. Opportunity may arise for such comments as: "When things go bad at home, kids are sometimes angry enough to fight anyone." "Maybe when you're being my assistant it keeps you from being with the group." Messages should be phrased, whenever possible, so as not to increase anxiety to a point of therapeutic immobilization. The therapist can use these statements as springboards for group discussion by asking for reasons why a child might be behaving or feeling as observed.

House Rules and Group Limits

Within stage II, a simple statement of house rules and limits is made. House rules are for the operational needs of the agency: tell the receptionist you are here and wait in the waiting room; we do not destroy property, run in the halls, go in the stairways, play with the fire boxes, elevators, or telephones. Group limits are imposed by the therapist because of his or her philosophy, needs, and tolerance level. All therapists have limits to their endurance, learned quickly and often uncomfortably, in anxiety-provoking situations that children and adolescents elicit, especially in groups.

Some basic group limits are "We do not hurt other people or ourselves here; what happens in the group is for the group's information only." One therapist limits anything more than hand-wrestling; another limits only if a child picks up a scissors and starts running after another, or two gang up on one. Hurt may be defined as hurt feelings. Some therapists make swearing against the rules; however, for many children the therapist's energy may be better spent. Further limits can range from those stated in contracts—for example, points are taken away for interrupting another person—to those based on idiosyncratic therapist need, for example, "Because I don't like to start groups late, all children will come on time or not be admitted if late."

A statement about confidentiality usually occurs within the groups during early sessions. No matter how severe or bizarre the pathological material a member shares with the group, it should not be repeated at school, to the children's parents, or outside. Sometimes children are told they can discuss the material with their parents or individual therapist when they need to unload but must not mention the name of the child. Children must also be assured by the therapist that he or she will not repeat confidential material to the parents. Confidentiality is an easier concept for older and better-functioning children to respect. Refusal to respect this is viewed by some therapists as reason for dismissal from the group. If violations occur, feelings about it can be discussed and handled as a group issue.

Rooms and equipment, often by their size, nature, and arrangement, can set physical and spatial controls. These can aid in self-control and reduce adult-imposed limits (Churchill, 1959). Selection of certain activities, such as finger painting, is contraindicated when doing ego-supportive treatment with other than inhibited children unless the agency has a very supportive maintenance crew.

Children's Initial Reactions

Initially, the therapist may assume that the children are reacting to him or her and to the other children in a pattern that is ego-syntonic for them. The pattern has been functional for the child and will probably occur in structured and nonstructured groups. These patterns, often given "game-playing" names, need individualized appraisal.

"Mother's helper" conveys "I am a good child and I don't need to be here," or "I will make you love me more than you love the others." An unwary therapist may find himself or herself with a "teacher's pet" or a "therapist's assistant."

The child whose behaviors seem to say, "I'm not here," plays a waiting game with the therapist. The child may be anxious or passive-aggressive. Anxiety requires consistent recognition and support from the therapist: Passive-aggressiveness often responds best to peers rather than to the therapist, whose comments can be interpreted as demands. With this child, clarification and interpretation involving the entire group may entice him or her from this stance.

A child whose initial approach is "Let's see you handle this!" tests the therapist immediately. It is a battle-cry from a child who perceives life as a struggle of power and control over the monster within him or her and those without. This child can be a powerful catalyst for group interaction because he or she precipitates expression of feelings hidden in other children.

The child who seems to say, "I need you more than those guys do," is often the most regressed member of the group. He or she allies himself with the therapist or with peers and may display jealousy when attention is paid to others.

The child who is involved in multiple-therapeutic contacts often walks into the group with more sophisticated expectations than the others. He may be set to play out certain conflicts over trust, power, and control that have developed in his or her other treatment contacts. The issues that arise necessitate clear communication about this child among the professionals concerned. This child may try to offend by describing how much "better or more interesting Dr. X's group was." This child is a valuable asset because he or she can verbally model for the other children and is often the most willing to begin communication.

Some children with rigid defenses approach group therapy intending to maintain control by behaving as if the situation were identical to home or school. One of the manifestations of this is semantic loading: This child is the last to give up calling the therapist "teacher." More subtly, he or she reacts to situations with little flexibility and accepts little support.

Goal Development

Individual goals become group goals as members begin to verbalize their desire to change. Levine (1979) points out that the individual must feel that his goals can and will be incorporated into the group goals (p. 111). Many children are unable as yet to share verbally, so the therapist may mention some children's individual goals and how they might become group goals. The therapist's goals are that the group can learn to listen to each other, to take turns, and to share their experiences. As members verbalize goals, the therapist helps facilitate group goal development. As these individual and group goals become the focus of therapeutic work, they become the nuclei of group decision-making and change. Mann (1955) points out that the primary goal of any group is group unity for the purpose of mutual exploration and solution of problems.

REFERENCES

Berkovitz, I. H. (1972). On growing a group: Some thoughts on structure, process, and setting. In I. H. Berkovitz (Ed.), *Adolescents grow in groups*, New York: Brunner/Mazel. pp. 6–30.

Bracklemanns, W. E., & Berkovitz, I. H. (1972). Younger adolescents in group psychotherapy: A reparative superego experience. In I. H. Berkovitz (Ed.), *Adolescents grow in groups*, New York: Brunner/Mazel. pp. 37–48.

Churchill, S. R. (1959). Prestructuring group content. *Social Work*, 4, 52–59.

Clifford, M., & Cross, T. (1980). Group therapy for seriously disturbed boys in residential treatment. *Child Welfare*, 59, 560–565.

Ganter, G., Yeakel, M., & Polansky, N. A. (1967). *Retrieval from limbo: The intermediary group treatment of inaccessible children*. New York: Child Welfare League of America.

Levine, B. (1979). *Group psychotherapy practice and development*. Englewood Cliffs, NJ: Prentice-Hall.

Mann, J. (1955). Some theoretic concepts of the group process. *International Journal of Group Psychotherapy*, 5, 235-241.

Redl, F., & Wineman, D. (1957) *The aggressive child*. New York: Free Press.

Rose, S. D. (1972). *Treating children in groups: A behavioral approach*. San Francisco: Jossey-Bass.

Sarri, R. C., & Galinsky, M. J. (1974). A conceptual framework for group development. In P. Glasser, R. Sarri, & R. Vinter (Eds.), *In-

dividual change through small groups. New York: Free Press. pp. 71–88

Schachter, R. S. (1974). Kinetic psychotherapy in the treatment of children. *American Journal of Psychotherapy, 28*, 430–437.

Schacter, R. S. (1984). Kinetic psychotherapy in the treatment of depression in latency age children. *International Journal of Group Psychotherapy, 34*, 83–91.

Slavson, S. R., & Schiffer, M. (1975). *Group psychotherapies for children.* New York: International Universities Press.

Sugar, M. (1974). Interpretive group psychotherapy with latency children. *Journal of the American Academy of Child Psychiatry, 13*, 648–666.

Chapter 5

STAGE III: ANXIETY

Laura H. Lewis

EXPERIENTIAL DESCRIPTION

It is as though the group has been awaiting a signal, and as soon as the stage II labeling identity occurs, the group reacts singly, by pairs, or in threesomes. The key words from here on are activity and action. There seems to be constant movement, both external and internal, and sound in steadily increasing volume. Voices are shrill and loud, but the sudden silences are equally loud. There are frequent comings and goings into and out of the group. A pair forms that closes everyone out, quickly dissolves, only to reform in different pairs. A child comes in close only to move his chair away, while another turns his back and covers his face. Still another opens expectantly and moves to meet the warmth only to flee at any move to approach him. The therapist moves from one to two and back as though shepherding leaves in a wind. He holds and works with one or two, only to leave them to entice or rescue another. He sets limits, only to wonder at the need with these changelings and their mercurial natures. He now appears "the therapist," then seemingly disappears in the group. There is little resemblance to a group and group process, little difference between patients and therapist. Existing is just the sense of movement, sound, and feeling, constantly moving to a crescendo.

The children seem to be continuously questioning everyone without asking. "Do you know I'm here? Where are the limits? Will you control me? Are you strong enough? Do you care enough? When or will you change?" It is a stage of dramatic individuality but with each seeking answers to similar questions with ever rising anxiety. It is a bad scene for the therapist, especially the initiate. It is filled with confusion and bewilderment, often despair and flashes of anger. The questions can be only fleetingly seen, never fully revealed or comprehended, lost in the swirl and flurry of activity and clouded by the intense anxiety rampant in the room. The therapist is now on trial, feels so, and often reacts to this, further clouding the issues.

Early excursions and explosions are met by the therapist's peers and the agency jokingly, later pointedly, "What kind of group are you running?" "Can you do something about the noise?" Finally, "Keep those kids in the room" comes from the agency. While dealing with his own anxieties and doubts, the therapist must endlessly respond to the child and the group with "Yes, I care enough. I am strong enough." At the same moment he must placate the scoffers and the authority while losing none of his self-confidence. In despair he can only ask, "Why do they not hear? Why will they not let me in? Will the group ever jell? Can I do it?"

Slowly, almost imperceptibly, a pattern begins to emerge unbeknownst to any of the combatants, for the tempo, intensity, and sound often increase. Asking the question, "Do you care enough?" or hearing an answer even on a superficial level, triggers even more intense anxiety necessitating flight into either withdrawal, silence, physically leaving, or wild acting out. The flight works. Anxiety drops. A new anxiety rises as to whether one has lost one's place. This precipitates flight to check it out. Then the whole sequence starts again with ever higher anxiety aimed at the therapist, building to a climax.

Somewhere in the kaleidoscope of movement about the therapist the same procedure begins between child and child or between child and subgroup. Slowly the "Yes" answer is heard on a deeper level. The children confine movement to the therapy room and begin the testing of this new truth. The anxiety never seems to drop. Pathological defenses are universal; they break often and easily under the constant stress. Conflicts are raw and blatant, acting out is wild and primitive, content is pathological and bizarre, and regressive behaviors appear.

Now children react singly and as a group to any changes. Absences of members are met with exaggerated fear, worry, guilt, and blame. Changes in time result in wild accusations and recriminations hurled into the group space to home in on the therapist. He feels it and reacts intensely and very often with anger. He may try new ways of conveying the answer, but finally in desperation he shouts, "Yes, I *am* strong enough. I am the therapist. I *can* control you and I will not let anyone be hurt." This is met with obvious relief by all the children, although it is still being tested. A subtle change has come. A group is in process of becoming. At the moment, it is evidenced through its growing importance to the child.

Through this time the universal question "Can you handle me?" becomes "You can handle me." Questioning changes. Although still primarily for the therapist, it is now also for the group. As nonspecific group roles are tried and abandoned, others are assumed or assigned. "How do I relate to others?" Answers are being heard by one here and another there. Although there is but little perceptible drop in activity, group internalization begins in a few children. They, in turn, begin demanding that others change. This precipitates wild anxiety as universally they demand, "How much do I have to change to stay here?"

Gradually, as each question climaxes in an answer, the child feels safe enough to feel slightly more committed. He now trusts enough to ask, "Can you help me?" but may not stay to hear the answer. It is as though this child now sees and feels dimly that he has a problem but has little real acknowledgment of it or commitment to seek change. The children reach this point singly and with great variability in timing.

The therapist may feel the change but often misses the inclusion of other group members in the focus of questioning and testing, noting only the speedup in questions needing answers. His discouragement is most intense at this point. His anxiety is increased from two external sources, for not only has the agency become insistent on control but the parents are being heard from. "What is happening to my child?" Some parents express delight over the child's improved behavior at home and suggest they'd like to withdraw. Another parent irately insists that his child has become much worse and is acting out at home and in school. He too threatens to withdraw the child. Still other parents insist on the therapist's time for their own anxieties, further burdening him.

The therapist wearies of handling both parents and children and of placating the agency; fearing he will never be heard, believed, and trusted, he becomes discouraged with the seeming lack of growth of group process. The fury still being raised by the laggards overshadows the progress of the few.

The advance guard in the group often adds to the melee by anger at the therapist for not "doing something about this mess." Finally, out of sheer desperation and with the sure feeling that it is now or never, the therapist insists with little finesse but with great finality, "This is *enough*. We will calm down. You will stay with us. We will talk about it. We will make some rules for our group. *Now!*" One or two will now direct their anger at the other members and demand, "Say, you guys, let's move on." With relief the therapist moves to help the process along.

Trust now appears openly and seems to grow more quickly. Noise begins to abate. Anxiety lessens. Warmth can creep in if it does so unobtrusively and is tolerated for a moment or two. Often in a flurry of activity and motion, the acknowledgment "You can help me" is heard. Rapidly, with obvious relief, the group becomes *our* group, the therapist becomes *our* therapist. The group slides into the next stage.

DYNAMIC DESCRIPTION

The goal for stage III is to move the children into an awareness of group process to an understanding of group therapy, and a beginning internalization of the group. A successful passage through this stage is a must for a successful treatment process in a group. The *anxiety stage* is the crucial stage in the life of group that marks the point of no return. It can be resolved in only two ways: either into the formation of a treatment group or to dissolution. If stage III is examined other than experientially, three phases emerge, revealing differing individual and group foci and goals.

Phase one begins with the initial surge of anxiety and remains focused throughout by the individual child on his or her relationship with the therapist. The child's goal is to interact with the therapist and to exclude the other children. The therapeutic goal for this phase is to help the child form a more solid, trusting relationship with the therapist.

Phase two begins when the child realizes that to keep and solidify his relationship with his important therapist, he must come to terms with his rivals, the other children. He begins to form a relationship with the others while continuing to test the therapist by testing limits, seeking strength and control, and revealing his pathology to the therapist. Phase two ends as the child attains a relationship with the other children and begins to recognize a similar relationship between the other children and the therapist.

In phase three the child is beginning to internalize the group and recognize that this group and membership in it are becoming desirable. This forces an awareness that he or she must change in order to maintain this membership. Phase three and stage III end when the child capitulates, accepts controls, and commits himself to group membership.

The Child

Individuality is the keymark of phase one. This individuality is different from seeing children as individuals in the group as observed in stage II. This individuality is glaring and constantly accented as the child's increasing anxiety and his struggle to resolve his ambivalence strain the coping mechanisms in his customary reaction patterns. Each move the child makes toward the therapist sends him flying one way or another. Each reassurance he hears moves him nearer the therapist into more anxiety. This rise in individual anxiety is one of the surest signs that stage III has begun.

This anxiety-producing process is revealed in behavior that is provocative, manipulative, possessive, demanding, rude, boisterous, active, protective, polite, subservient, placating, testing, or whining. The child may join another child to ward off the therapist or his own feelings, may collude with another child against a third, may struggle for dominance and leadership, or may scapegoat. The intent of the behavior is the same: to escape, to dilute, or to destroy the closer relationship with the therapist, to drive the other children away from himself and the therapist, or to join with them to exclude the therapist. Yet the child is trapped in the situation by his or her own needs. He or she needs, wants, and seeks the affective nurturance offered. He or she fears, avoids, and flees it because it means intimacy and change. Fearing the loss of what he or she has already attained, the child tried to relieve it by running back to the therapist only to begin again. A true approach-avoidance situation exists.

The data the child seeks are those that allow him to explore, define, and test the emotional boundaries of the therapist's relationship to him. With each new confirmed bit of information, the child must re-form hypotheses and collect more data. He asks again for control by testing the strength of the therapist more actively. He is relieved if an answer is quickly available, for at best his knowledge is shaky, and he constantly checks, refutes, accepts, and rechecks it all again. Gradually, the child becomes more aware of his worth to the therapist. At this point, he has gained some relief from struggling to and from the therapist, and the relationship has grown in importance and comfort. Although the child's anxiety is still intense, it is less so when he is near the therapist, so he struggles to stay in the room. Staying usually decreases fear of loss.

Up to phase two, the child has amassed considerable data about the other group members, having progressed from seeing them as objects who are different yet similar to learning that the group and group time is shared with them. Depending on the age, nature and degree of disturbance, children vary in their ability to see and relate to the other children as real objects. Healthier children with latency development are able to observe and relate to the others in dyads and small groupings, viewing the other children as need-satisfiers and identification models.

At times these peer relationships are an even more important focus than their relationship with the therapist. With younger and more severely disturbed children, the other members have remained relatively unimportant, largely accepted as necessary to the setting in which the child relates to the therapist. Now the child must begin at a different level to deal with the others. A new source of anxiety, rivalrous feelings, often emerges full blast. Efforts to eliminate his or her rivals brings information that this is not an acceptable part of the game. The child realizes that he must also find some way to live with these peers. This process begins afresh, one at a time with his group peers, at approximately the same relationship level that he had with the therapist at the beginning of stage III.

Phase two has begun, and the child's anxiety now never seems to abate. He begins to reveal intentionally how bad the situation is within him while also checking out his safety in a relationship with his peers. His defense mechanisms are rarely up to the strain, and the results depend considerably on the nature, depth, and pervasiveness of his pathology. Internal and external conflicts are blatant. Content of speech and behavior may by pathological and bizarre.

Rarely does a single child use all of these behaviors, but he or she will use several within a single session or from session to session. It can be a confusing scene of wild acting out, noise, confusion, and pressure as the child and his fellows push the therapist for control and strength. This is the group's and the child's most difficult time to date, and the demands for support, reassurance, caring, and control appear insatiable. Support and reassurance are offered by the therapist, followed by some of the peers. Amazingly, with little external evidence, the child uses it to the degree to which he or she is capable.

It is difficult to assess the actual progress of a single child. Each of the children is following a similar process. Several will be at the same point at the same time. It is difficult to pinpoint when a child accepts support from a peer or when he offers it to another. Very subtly and slowly, the child forms a relationship with another child. Slowly he or she recognizes similar relationships among the group, as these children have begun to grow in worth to each other.

Overt signs of the beginning of phase three will be hearing the use of group pronouns. First appearing as labels, "our time," "our room," are used outside of the group with the receptionist, parents, or other children en route to the therapy room. The individual child begins to react to absences and changes in routine. As the group and group members begin growing in importance to the child, internalization of the group begins.

It has become evident that change must occur in order to be group members. As this idea is submitted to the same checking as every other idea, the group process is well on its way in a child. This new feeling is both attractive and frightening, but it seems to offer a way of resolving the conflict. As it is sought, impatience and anger are directed at those impending its growth. It is often a child or several children who demand limits and strict rules to bring the group under control. The tempo in the group has reached almost unbearable heights.

When the therapist, with great resolve and firmness, asserts control by restating the group purpose, the child's and group's reactions are immediate and observable. As the therapist shares his desire that they all continue working toward these goals, each joins openly, demanding all conform. It is clear they all have shared this wish and have each been involved in the need for controls. As order emerges out of chaos, there is delight in shared feelings—*our* therapist, *our* group. The new group entity is explored with each child prepared and committed to go on in the discovery of group membership. The anxiety stage ends.

The Therapist

The novice and the experienced therapist alike move into stage III using their individual relationship with the child to help form relationships between the children, to foster the group relationship, and to begin the group work. They are chagrined and startled to discover the children are not ready for all this and dismayed with the wild rise in anxiety. Intuitively moving to buffer and control the anxiety frequently results in the therapist becoming fatigued and empty before he or she realizes the children are not making use of the help. The anxiety continues unabated and the children begin acting it out.

The experienced therapist recognizes grimly that the anxiety stage has begun and settles to work it out. He works to solidify the relationship of the individual child to him, using every opportunity to explain the feelings and motives of the children to each other. He plans his strategy hoping he does not succumb to the anxiety or become too drained to function effectively. Building up his own support system he determines this time to end this stage a little sooner. Sometimes he is able to do so and sometimes not. He has techniques with which he is comfortable and skilled for handling the work during this stage. However, he is still uneasy. With children, interactions and relationships are on a very real, intense level, necessitating honest, straight nonverbal and verbal messages. It is tricky to build trust with a disturbed child; the therapist must "feel" through each interaction and relationship himself as well as empathizing with the child. This demands a great deal from the therapist as a therapist and as a person.

No matter how many times a therapist lives through stage III with a group, he or she is always startled to re-live the feelings of the first time: fatigue, despair, confusion, fear, anger, pain, and much self-doubt. It is not a surprise that this stage demands hard work and much investment, but the intensity of the feelings is sometimes unnerving, especially anger at the children individually and collectively. Because of this intensity, the high activity and noise level, and the blatant pathology, it is nearly impossible to keep a clear picture of what is occurring as it is happening. This leads to self-doubt, because the therapist fears that his timing or ability to read the children and their progress is off the mark. Perhaps this will be the group that he cannot help through this stage.

It is crucial that the therapist be aware of the effect that pressure, from external sources and from practical matters, can have on him and on his feelings toward and about the group, and how these pressures can change his handling of the group. Criticism is more prevalent from all these sources during this stage. If job security and pointed attacks on the therapist's ability, clinical judgment, and technique are added, his or her confidence and ability can be badly shaken at a time when both are in constant demand.

The first time a therapist encounters the anxiety stage is an experience unlikely to be forgotten. All of those things noted for the experienced therapist are true for the initiate, only more so. Even forewarned, it is not possible truly to prepare for this stage. More than one therapist has been "turned off" groups for some time, some never to reexperience them. Bringing a group through this stage can be a very rewarding experience. Therapists can gain considerable self-knowledge and demonstrate that they can help and control a group, while feeling with the children and using themselves therapeutically.

The emphasis and interpretation the therapist gives the children and group vary, based on the differing sources of anxiety in each phase. Phase one messages are concerned with increasing trust in the therapist, the child knowing that the therapist sees and accepts him. "It's okay to be mad, but I see it frightens you." The therapist individualizes the messages, determining when information is sought and needed and when maneuvers are defensive.

In phase two these messages continue, often in the face of wild acting out and testing of control. The child will need reassurance about his pathology, his "badness," for he now lets it all hang out and must know that the therapist sees this and continues to accept him. As the phase progresses it becomes necessary to step up the interpretations of the feelings, intent, and wishes of the other group members in order to foster relationships between the children and to lead them toward group commitment.

Phase three shows children exhibiting blatant psychopathology, such as distortion of reality, open fantasy, hallucinations, and other bizarre behavior. Pathological rage or grief, the destructive impulses and their intensity, which are so often a part of the severely disturbed child's inner dynamics, arouse naked fear and anxiety in the children and sometimes even in the therapist. If the therapist is prepared to accept such reactions in himself, he can more easily continue to care for, accept, and control the disturbed child while helping the other children handle it to their therapeutic advantage.

The messages become more and more centered on the group, group process, and group feelings in the third phase, with the therapist consciously dropping the singular personal pronouns and stressing "we" and "us." When anxieties arise from the need to make a commitment to the group, both therapist and group members aid each child.

The Group

Group formation and group process is difficult to see in stage II and the early phases of stage III, but it becomes somewhat clearer as stage III progresses. At the beginning of stage III the child's perception of the therapist is incomplete. As the relationship with the therapist grows in importance, the child's awareness and perception of him and of the other children undergo subtle changes. The child becomes aware of the rivalry, and early in phase two the interactions between child and child are mostly negative. Both positive communications and feedback between children are filtered through the therapist. The children begin to build a line of communication tentatively but directly between one another, following the lead of the therapist. Slowly, trust grows in the group, the outward signs being their use of group pronouns, reactions to absences, and concern for each other.

Phase three has begun, as has internalization of the group process. Considerable activity is being seen between pairings and threesomes, with changing in the groupings. Talking about *our group* is heard, as solid relationships exist between the children and the therapist. The anxiety stage is coming to an end as trust is becoming stronger.

The Parents

At the beginning of stage III, some parents have reached an uneasy peace or a wait-and-see attitude. Some, because of their own pathology, symbiosis with their child, need for a family scapegoat, or disagreement with their spouse, may be waiting a more propitious time for making their feelings and wishes known. It cannot be too strongly stressed that anything that touches the dynamic web uniting a family causes a reaction, like a ripple, affecting each member. These ripples increase in intensity and strength in stage III and portend, with dramatic intensity, change within the family. It is not possible to change any family member dynamically without affecting every other family member. As the child's anxiety and changes in behavior are dramatic in stage III, the flood reaches the family, bringing about an anxiety reaction. Even more dramatic is the recognition of what is yet to come. The family and child begin to experience changes in the family-dynamic relationships and communication system.

Change that is already occurring in the child in phase one often appears at home as a reversal of the child's customary patterns of behavior. The very good child may now act out at home or school. The acting-out youngster may confine his or her acting out to the group setting and cease to do so elsewhere. The very depressed child may become hostile, argumentative, and irritable. The overdependent, symbiotic child may begin subtly resisting the symbiosis, making moves toward independence. In any of these situations either a conscious or intuitive recognition of these occurrences triggers a rise in parental concern. This rise is as sharp but possibly not as intense as is the child's rise in anxiety at the beginning of stage III. Since parents lag somewhat behind the child, phase one may be nearing its end before the parents' anxiety is elevated to the point that they begin offering feedback to the therapist by seeking him or her out more frequently.

Very often this feedback comes as positive statements about the changes in the child that the therapist may find unbelievable. In some instances the parents are honestly quite pleased and may be only seeking verification that their child is indeed better. Some realize that the hostility or acting out may be real progress, a move toward well-rounded functioning. They then innocently inquire as to how much longer therapy must continue. Other parents are not sure they really want their child like this; or they claim the child is well and needs no more therapy, and they want to withdraw.

Other parents report that their child has become much worse, acting out at home and/or school. He is moody, cries, is irritable, or any of the dozen reactions the parents see as worse. There is the frightened, concerned parent who asks, "What's happening? Will he stay this way? Was he always this sick? Is he crazy?" The parent who irately demands to know what the therapist is doing for the child is worse; he or she threatens immediate withdrawal. The pathological parent who reports the same behavior and demands something from the therapist is asking for help with his or her own anxieties, demanding, caring and attention from the therapist. Still other disturbed parents carefully sabotage any therapeutic effort to help their child while continuing to keep the child in the group.

The need is the same. The parent must be helped with his or her anxieties, helped to build more trust, rapport, and commitment to the therapist either directly with him or through his agent. Parents must trust the therapist's ability, ethics, and techniques enough to allow their child to continue with concomitant changes in the child, the family, and the parents themselves. They need to be taught about group process and progress. They may now or later need direct counseling in the changes necessary in themselves and their handling of the child, and those needed in the family to foster change in the child or to ensure that it lasts. These approaches need to be offered and the parents helped to accept them, whether the child's change is positive or negative, whether the parents are disturbed or stable.

This is a crucial point in the group. The parents' needs, expectancies, and concerns are real and of legitimate concern to the therapist. If the parent cannot build a more solid relationship with the therapist, making the transition through stage III, then the child rarely can do so. The parents must recommit themselves to change in their child and must free the child to make this change. On occasion it is possible for a child to be motivated and strong enough to do so without actually being freed by the parent and family. Late latency-age children or adolescents can occasionally do so, but it is an extremely rare occurrence in younger children.

The Agency

The anxiety stage is the most difficult stage for the agency, just as it is for the persons more intimately involved with the group, with parallel anxieties rising high. The therapist and the agency authorities must keep this in mind and take care to keep communication open. The therapist must be well aware of the agency's limits on destructive, disruptive behavior and the contingencies set on breaking these limits, and must operate within them. It is often at the agency's insistence that the therapist acts to end this stage, optimally timed by the progress of the children.

SPECIAL ISSUES

Handling Anxiety

The anxiety of stage III is individual and unique, yet contagious and universal. This anxiety and its containment, buffering, and channeling will concern the therapist throughout the stage. The therapist realizes that the child hears or comprehends very little of what is conveyed to him, either verbally or feelingly, when he is highly anxious. Each therapist has his or her own special way or handling anxiety but in general seeks to lower it to a tolerable level and at the same time turn his and the child's attention to its source in an effort to bring a resolution of the conflict that underlies it. The same techniques for relieving anxiety are used regardless of its source, but the interpretative message the child needs varies with the nature of the underlying conflict.

Nonverbally, the therapist needs to be open to the child, aware of and concerned for him, yet giving a feeling of strength, patience, and positive acceptance. Verbally, the therapist acknowledges the child's fear and anxiety and offers him or her support with the feelings. In addition, the therapist reassures the child that he need not move more rapidly than he can tolerate. The child needs to know repeatedly that the therapist does understand or will not stop until he does, and that the therapist is certain that with help the child can handle his problems.

Messages must be honest, succinct, and phrased in language that the child can understand. If too much verbiage or too sophisticated language is used, it may increase the anxiety and interfere with the child's hearing the message. At first the therapist can be reassuring. "I can help." "You don't need to rush."

"You can calm down." "It's okay to be afraid." "I see how you feel." "I do understand." "I won't change." Gradually, the messages are changed, and therapist and child enter the "Yes, but" period of the stage. The message now goes something like this: "Yes, I know you are afraid, but you can stay here." "Yes, I see that, but we can talk about it."

Very often in stage III messages are ineffective, for the child cannot use them. The therapist must use reassurance, and help in times of increased stress. The therapist learns as soon as possible to recognize quickly the times when the child cannot accept help of this kind. At these times, the therapist may need simply to turn his own and the group's attention from this child to allow him the time he needs to accept the messages. If the child's behavior is destructive to the group, the therapist may suggest a "time out period for cooling off" and allow the child to withdraw to a corner of the room. If this is ineffective or if the anxiety too high, the child can be permitted to leave the room. If the situation is adroitly handled, the child gains the relief he needs and is able to return to the group. In the use of such a measure, the therapist needs to present it matter-of-factly and firmly, yet with readily apparent acceptance of the child's need for help. A physically abusive child should be handled immediately without courting the danger of physical harm to another child or to himself.

The technique for use of the cooling-off period outside of the room is as follows. A worker who knows the children should be available and should remain in the hall during this stage of the group. When the need arises, the therapist communicates to worker and child in this manner: "Eric has been having a hard time and needs a chance to sit quietly for a while. About two minutes will probably do it, right, Eric? When things ease a little, we'll be glad to have you with us." The child remains with the worker or, as appropriate, with a co-therapist in the hall. Any conversation should be neutral and not about group work. The worker helps and reinforces the child's return to group. If the timing is such that the child does not return before the session ends, the therapist will spend time with him, preferably while other members are still around. When this occurs for the first time, adequate explanation and reassurance need to be made to the group and the resulting reactions handled at once.

It cannot be mentioned too frequently that this is a difficult and trying stage for the therapist. The situation can become clouded and neary incomprehensible when there are four to eight disturbed, intensely anxious children, all clammering for the therapist, his attention, and his caring at the same time. If the therapist is anxious or "catches" the children's anxiety, the situation may become nearly intolerable. If the therapist is unaware of or loses sight of the fact that each measure of help that lowers the child's anxiety moves the child closer to the source of the anxiety, causing it to rise again, he may assume that he is failing, that the children are too sick, that he lacks the skill to pull it off, or that he is making the child worse. However, if he can accept that anxiety, fatigue, and despair are natural reactions to this very difficult time, he may find his own anxiety dropping and be better able to cope with the situation.

Testing Limits and Acting-Out Behavior

Acting out and testing of limits are an ever-present accompaniment to this action, noise-oriented stage. These behaviors are seen throughout but change somewhat from phase to phase. It is important to differentiate between acceptable and unacceptable activity, testing of limits, struggles for control, and acting out of feelings, impulses, fantasies, and conflicts. Although the control measures needed may be very similar, the interpretations and messages the child or children need can be quite different.

Physical activity is an acceptable accompaniment of childhood. To expect a child to sit still and take part in a spontaneous discussion without extraneous movement is a nonsensical expectation. In general, children's activity does not interfere with concentration and participation if it is suitably channeled for the situation and providing the activity is an extraneous accompaniment and not a project in itself. In the therapy room, activity needs will be defined by the chronological and developmental ages of children, and the acceptable level of activity will be defined by the tolerance levels of both therapist and group members. Unacceptable activity is that which is judged to be a hindrance to the child's group participation and an interference with his or others' concentration and participation, causing an interference or disruption in group progress. It is this unacceptable activity that is to be controlled.

Many children convert anxiety into activity, and as anxiety increases in this stage, the tempo of activity and noise picks up also. The children may be unable to remain in chairs, continually roaming the room; they may move in their chairs, make noise, talk incessantly, play with fingers, chairs, or clothing. If the activity is an expression of anxiety, relieving the anxiety will usually help curtail the activity and allow them to channel their activity in group-acceptable ways.

Some of this apparently aimless activity can be determined as more goal-oriented and less expressive of anxiety. In some of the instances, it may be a subtle testing of limits as a part of the child's data collection about the therapist, to determine if the therapist is aware of the child, if he or she will maintain limits, and how sharp the therapist is. This tentative try at testing may be the only attempt the child makes; however, in many cases it is simply a warning of a real struggle for control yet to come. Some children have a pathological need to control every interaction they encounter and in this way ward off close relationships, frustrate the adult, and reject any effort to help them.

Acting-out behavior refers to a loss of control by the child and his conversion, of feeling—anxiety, fear, anger, or depression—into action expressed in such a way that it it emotionally or physically harmful to himself, other children, or the therapist. Acting out is to be expected and anticipated in therapeutic groups of children. It is this acting-out behavior for which control is needed. This is an area in which many therapists feel frustration and failure, as they believe they "can't control" the children. The goal is not to stamp out the expression of the feeling but only to channel the expression in such a way that it can be worked with to therapeutic advantage. A balance of control, limits, and allowing expression through activity needs to be achieved. The therapist's personal and theoretical framework will determine the limits he sets for the children in both types of acting out.

Diligent work with a co-therapist and consultant needs to be done in order to be prepared for the steps of control necessary during this stage. The therapist's feelings, attitude, and reactions to control and its institution in the group are crucial elements in preparing for this stage. Spontaneous grabbing, restraining, or ejecting a child in the heat of a conflict could be disastrous and might cost the child and group much time in backtracking in order to reestablish trust. Well planned and thought-out techniques and progressive steps of control need to be understood and available to the therapist. These steps also need to be clearly discussed and understood by the group before the necessity for instituting them arises, or at least at the time the first need for them arises.

These techniques for the control of acting-out behavior are similar regardless of its source, but the timing and the message the child needs varies with the underlying dynamics and feelings. There are points of no return where intervention is needed and the therapist cannot hesitate to institute controls. He will begin very often with an effort to keep the child verbally, somewhat in this manner: "I understand your feelings, but I cannot allow you to do that"; "Stop it, Scott! You cannot do that here." If the child has been unable to do more than partially respond, and verbal control is not enough, a hand on the shoulder or arm can be added. "You can talk it out and keep yourself from hitting." When mild restraint in addition to positive, reassuring measures is ineffective, the child may be placed to one side of the room to regain control. Further progressive steps may include taking him from the room for a cooling-off period or removing him to a quiet room or freedom room. Much reassurance and supportive messages, indicating that it is okay to need such help, are given to the child and to the group. Exclusion from the group for the remainder of the session is a final step.

In the use of any of these techniques, the child must hear and be helped to feel that neither therapist nor group rejects him or feels that he is bad. They see and accept him apart from what he does, yet he will be controlled and stopped from hurting and totally disrupting the group. Sometimes children like to set up rules during this stage to help ensure enforcement and add clout. By accepting control from the therapist and group, gradually the child learns he can control himself. It takes infinite patience and constant vigilance to detect the problem, move at the right time, and deliver the message so that the child can use it.

Some children and groups respond more favorably to one or another of the methods, depending on their dynamics and previous experiences. Whether to allow more time, to restrain, or to provide distance, as a means of supporting the ego's control mechanisms, is the crucial decision. The therapist's judgment and theoretical orientation determine which and when to implement. The child with little impulse control cannot work with the same leeway others have. There is also the child who initially needs slightly longer to meet limits or the one who is so inhibited that acting out may be encouraged. If the group shows intolerance of these differences, the therapist should reevaluate the situation to be sure that his judgment is sound and that he has not "been had."

Care must be taken that the child does not go beyond what is a therapeutic leeway or continue beyond the actual need. Younger children and latency-age children sometimes respond well to being held in order to control aggressive attacks on others or destructive attacks on property. But specific care must be taken that children not feel they need to act out to be held or to get other attention. Acting out can be "catching," with children "following the leader" for some sort of attention, trying it out for themselves before the need to use it arises. One must be alert for cases of one child or the entire group acting out for another. As all of the children must share the therapist, new methods need to be tried if any single child requires holding a majority of the time. Holding some children is not advisable, as it can become too stimulating to the child and can be experienced as a sexual or aggressive approach. More often than not it is not experienced as calming. Judgment, history, and experience help to identify these children.

Some groups must be carefully structured from the beginning. Controls and measures for enforcing them are then spelled out carefully before and in the first session. Examples of such groups are aggressively acting-out adolescents and older latency-age children and severely disturbed children. These groups are prevented from structuring their own controls because of the expression of their pathology or developmental task. Activities and games also can be utilized. These groups may be more accepting of consequences and controls if they were incorporated into the initial contract. As adolescence brings with it the developmental task of resolving authority conflicts, a group can find itself in the midst of a "no win" situation unless these conflicts can be avoided from the beginning by this careful structuring. A mutual and specific contract, spelling out responsibilities, house rules, and contingencies, may be made before the first session. The therapist cannot choose for the child or group but can only insist that the contingency chosen be followed.

Children Presenting Special Difficulty

Not all children reach the zenith of the accomplishments expected during this stage, but is it imperative that each child make minimal changes in order to commit himself or herself to seek group membership and identity. Even the children who lag far behind their group mates must take these steps before they can end the anxiety stage. Among these laggards are children with intense resistances to change, those with repeated negative and painful experiences with relationships, and sometimes highly intelligent children who use their intellects to avoid relationships. Often seeming not to form any relationships until the others are almost through the stage, these children seem to profit greatly by the experiences of the others, learning vicariously by observing the relationship formation between their peers and the therapist. Children fearing a one-to-one relationship may be able to form the relationships necessary in the group due to the nature of the group setting. They experience the risks and losses involved in a group relationship as less intense than in a one-to-one and may utilize the process of splitting dependency needs between therapist and group or co-therapists. Pressure from the advanced guard in the group is often vociferous and helps to push them to take the risks necessary. The therapist will often "feel" the beginning relationship and find himself supporting the child by saying, often to his own amazement, "Tom is coming along; he'll be with us," or some similar statement.

Seriously disturbed children who have untold difficulties forming close relationships may lag far behind their fellows in the intensity levels of their relationship formation, sophistication of internalization of the group, and active participation in the group process. Such children can become accepted members of the group, take part in and use the group work to the degree they are able, and not necessarily impede the progress of the group. It is often noted that a relatively intact group of children will tolerate, accept, and help a seriously disturbed child while making quite sophisticated progress of their own. This child can make considerable progress with such a group even when it may be obvious that long-term individual therapy and additional group work are needed. Some groups, though, are unable to tolerate such a seriously disturbed child. Regressive or bizarre behaviors may be too threatening to them because they trigger their developmental or pathological conflicts. In this case, the child may need to be removed in order for the group to progress. This decision should be made only after it is clear that stage III is being unnecessarily prolonged and all others appear ready to move into stage IV.

Another type of child is found in those instances in which one youngster forms a collusion with another and uses this collusion actively to oppose relationship formation, group process, and progress. A collusion as it is used here refers to a pathological relationship between two children, maintained to obviate the need to change. These relationships may be shown in several ways: One of the pair may use the other for working out or acting out his or her feelings while seemingly remaining aloof; one may protect the other, may ward off any closeness with others, or may attempt to supply all dependency needs. Very often these children have been involved in such relationships with a parent or a sib and hence attempt to perpetuate the model. These collusions must be broken up, as these two children cannot change in it and it is unlikely that they will allow the remainder of the group to change. They need to be separated to help them function individually. Within the group, the children should be seated away from each other, with the weaker being next to the therapist. Then both should be encouraged to be separate individuals. There should be open discussion of their relationship as presenting a problem to the progression of the group, to be worked on in the group. Support, pressure, and suggestions frequently come from the rest of the group.

If separation and group pressure do not succeed sufficiently, the following may take place within the group, or outside, depending on the therapist's orientation. A thorough explanation needs to take place, giving a clear message that the relationship is harmful to the two and to the group's progress and that it cannot continue. Both children need support and reassurance to choose alternative ways of handling the situation, agreeing to break the collusion. Cues should be arranged to help the children see when they are moving into the old pattern. When this approach succeeds, there is clear evidence of it in the immediate drop in group anxiety and therapeutic movement in one or both of the two children. If one or both of the children is unable or refuses to break the pathological portion of the relationship, he or she will either choose to leave the group or be asked to do so by the therapist. If one leaves, the other will continue to need considerable support and guilt assuaging.

Dropouts

The attrition rate during stage III tends to be lower than for the preceding stage. Children leave spontaneously, fleeing from changing as much as appears necessary for them to stay or judging the cost of change too high. Their overwhelming anxiety may be the precipitant to flight. Other children who are not able to form the necessary close relationships to complete this stage may not drop out but instead need the therapist to make this decision. When this is necessary, the timing is important both to the individual child and to the group. The most advantageous time would appear to be before the end of phase two. It is unlikely that the novice therapist will detect these cases early enough to be prepared to handle them at this time. The experienced therapist also may wish to continue such children into phase three, hoping to break through to them and help them into the group. If this fails, these children must be dropped before phase three can be brought to a close.

The therapist must convey the decision to the group, immediately explaining simply and honestly what has happened. He will help them work through their anger, loss, and fear. Some children will be guilty, accepting responsibility for another child's leaving; others may become fearful, feeling that they may be next to go; and still others may act out, testing again whether the therapist can be trusted. The therapist must be alert during this time to pick up cues to these reactions in order to help the children. In some cases the other children are very much aware of the destructive aspects of the particular child's behavior; they may react to his or her discontinuing with relief and move directly into stage IV.

Making these decisions is usually quite difficult for the therapist, especially the first time. He will find himself experiencing many feelings about this, including grief, anger, loss, failure, despair, and relief. He may well spend some time reassessing the situation, feeling that he should have done something earlier or differently, to have enabled the child to continue. If he has done his best with the group, this is often a useless piece of self-indulgence, and he may need help from a consultant to resolve these feelings. He will then be free to handle the further recommendations for this child. The therapist may have to content himself with the thought that if he helps the child with this decision, the child may well be able to seek professional help at a more propitious time.

Adding New Group Members

In order to insure steady progress in the group it is better not to add new members after the beginning of stage III. It is clear that therapeutic progress is hampered and this stage unnecessarily prolonged if additions are made. It is not impossible to add a child at this time, if one is practicing in an agency that insists that a certain number be maintained for financial or political reasons. There are also some situations where one may decide for therapeutic reasons to add a new member, such as when a group needs a specific child to act as a catalyst for the group.

In preparing the group for a new member, the therapist must succinctly but clearly explain the reasons that necessitate such an addition. Sufficient time must be taken to allow the children individually and/or as a group to express and work on their anger, fear, and frustration at such a move. Adding the new child can become an excellent opportunity for moving the children into group decision-making and group action. If the children are well into phase three, this can be most profitable and also may help ensure only a relatively slight degree of regression; however, if the group is at the end of phase one or into phase two, there will be little chance of keeping them from regressing to the beginning of the stage. The work already accomplished will not be lost, although it will be hard to convince the novice therapist of this. The children generally work quickly through the steps already passed once the new child is accepted.

The selection of a child to add to an ongoing group is a tough one. A less disturbed, more intact child, who has some ability at relationship formation, would appear to have the strength needed to join a group of children whom he knows already know each other. One also should attempt to choose a child who could fill a group need. One must give careful attention to the child and his parents, so that they understand and accept the initial contract. The therapist also may feel the need to add some specifics to the child's contract regarding acceptance of the rules and limits that have been a product of the growth of the group to date. The therapist also may wish to spend some time building a relationship with the child slightly beyond the point he or she reached with each of the other members before beginning the group.

The group may be quite discouraged and drained after the first session including the new child. This will be especially so if the therapist is unprepared for the regression the "older" members may show. The therapist may feel "caught in the middle," trying to balance between including, supporting, and protecting the new member while reassuring, supporting, leading, and controlling the others. However, patience, and times are often all that are required for success.

Co-Therapists and Stage III

The anxiety stage accents very clearly and quickly all the salient arguments both pro and con for the use of co-therapists in group therapy with children. This stage is at least as difficult for two therapists as for one. Although all those factors that cause the individual therapist such fatigue, frustration, discouragement, and feelings of failure are present for co-therapists, there is someone with whom to share them. This sharing in itself may cause the therapist much difficulty, since many of the problems experienced by co-therapists arise from the relationship between the two and are intensified by stage III. Even co-therapists who have worked together previously can run into new difficulties during this stage.

One source of conflict can arise from a lack of understanding of what such a relationship entails, especially as to closeness, trust, openness, and investment. This is especially true for novice therapists. The pathology presented by the children and their modes of relating with adults puts an intense strain on the relationship between the therapists. Still other sources of conflict can be the differences in the individual tolerance for acting out, noise, activity, and pathology. These can lead to differences of opinion in any stage but arouse intense feelings during this stage as to what kinds of limits to set and when and how to set them. Wide differences between the therapists' tolerance levels for their own stress and anxiety and their reaction to these feelings in themselves can lead to difficulty.

Manipulative maneuvers aimed at dividing the therapists, pitting one against another, or claiming all of the attention of one are common behaviors employed by children during this stage with co-therapists. Sometimes this can reach scapegoating proportions by projecting all negative transference to one therapist, blaming him or her for all interferences, and refusing to relate to him or her. Occasionally the co-therapists have unwittingly allowed this due to the confusions and incomprehensiblity of this stage at times. At other times a child or the group may be acting out the unconscious conflicts of the co-therapists.

One therapeutic technique can be utilized in this stage by virtue of there being two therapists present. This situation often occurs spontaneously and is capitalized on by the therapists, but it also may be fostered if indicated. A child differentially uses the two therapists in resolving internal conflicts by dividing the conflicted feelings between the therapists. In this way, the child avoids the confusion of two contrary feelings for the same person. Examples of these conflicts are the need for nurturance versus the fear of closeness, a wish for closeness versus a fear of abandonment, a wish to be good and accepted versus rage at fear of rejection, and the oedipal conflict. When the conflicted feelings are understood, interpreted, and handled jointly by the therapists, the child is helped to discover that he can safely experience both positive and negative feelings for the same person, or that he can work on and resolve a conflict in a way he may not have been able to before.

Consultation and Supervision

Consultation and supervision during stage III are generally more active and challenging than in other stages. As the therapist is experiencing higher anxiety, frustration, fatigue, and despair, more help is needed to relieve these. The therapist needs support and encouragement during this stage, not questioning and criticism. As it is easy during this stage for the therapist to lose sight of the overall group process and progress, the consultant must be attentive to them, giving a great deal of information and recommending techniques.

The challenge and difficulty of consulting with co-therapists can be great due to the complexity of the parallel processes present and the propensity for conflict in areas of control and acting out during this stage. This stage brings out differences in technique, style, and personality, and any problem areas between the therapists will intensify and will require time to work out.

Length of the Stage

Stage III can be relatively short, several sessions, or several months. Important factors in the length of this stage are the composition, and core conflicts of the group and experience and skill level of the therapist. An experienced therapist recognizes quickly that this stage has begun and moves to handle anxiety, control the children, and teach them the steps of this stage, with confidence and patience to wait it out.

Groups will be prolonged during this stage when trust and control issues are central to the children's dynamics and reasons for initial referral. Acting-out children and those with authority conflicts will spend the majority of their total group time in this stage.

Often this stage is somewhat shorter with children who have had previous group or individual therapy experience. One observed phenomenon about inpatient groups and some day hospital groups, even with very disturbed children, is that the anxiety stage often does not seem as violent or prolonged. One could speculate that the overall level of control and the ability to have one's acting out dealt with therapeutically during most of one's day obviates much of it within the group.

Chapter 6

STAGE IV: COHESION

Christine S. Kandaras

EXPERIENTIAL DESCRIPTION

The group, individually and collectively, slides into stage IV with relief. Everyone and everything is quieter now, even the room appears more subdued. There is an awareness on everyone's part of this change in atmosphere. Frequent comments are: "Now I can hear myself think"; "It's about time you guys quieted down"; or "I like it better when everyone's not fighting." In this absence of group tension a sense of anticipation evolves—anticipation that now each child can be heard and can begin to verbalize, looking for solutions to their problems as a group. "Now we can really talk and help each other."

Anxiety is present but belongs to each child. It is no longer diffuse, free floating, nor threatening to disrupt the group. Each child struggles to bring forward his or her painful, pressing experiences for discussion and containment. Stories begin to spill out about deserting fathers, erratic mothers, violence, brothers who have died, and chaos that has reigned. The air is often heavy with depression. Gross exaggerations often appear in the stories, as the child reexperiences what has loomed inside so overpoweringly for so long. The therapist helps by pointing out how small and helpless the child must have felt at the time. He helps another child by careful structuring and reconstructing.

The other children are silent, sometimes deep into their own experiences, which have been triggered by the stories. The pervasive mood is felt and shared even if the particulars are not heard, as each child gets caught up with feelings inside. As the need arises in others to unload their long-kept stories, there is some jockeying for whose turn is next. A sense of fairness is strong, and group pressure grows to assure everyone's turn. Hesitant children are encouraged by the therapist and each other to share their experience. The therapist is more active in his role of relating feelings and experiences to behavior and defenses. An expectation develops that psychic pain will be lessened through this process.

Many groups have a member who likes to "grandstand" or perform. This child will tell dreadful stories about his or her life while the other children listen with horrid fascination. These stories are often believed by the others and can cause anxiety to rise enough to throw the group momentarily back into the anxiety stage. The therapist will try to catch this before it happens, by pointing out to the group what is happening. The performer usually stops when an interpretation is made by the therapist or when pressure is applied by the group.

Another member may be a stimulator for group discussion. He understands, intuitively perhaps, what is to come. To ensure himself a special place with the therapist, or perhaps simply because he is brighter or has had more therapy, this child will initiate discussions in the group and is ready to relate to other group members before they are ready to relate as a group. Often the others do not resent this but find it helpful. They do resent it, however, if it becomes apparent that this is a child who accurately pinpoints their feelings but does not look at his own.

The children's ability to verbalize their problems depends directly on their verbal skills, their ego intactness, their intellect, past therapy experience, their personalities, and their social backgrounds. Each child may repeat for himself and the therapist why he or she is in the group but is still somewhat embarrassed in front of the other children. There is shyness about some symptoms, such as bed-wetting, and boasting about others, such as getting kicked out of school. Yet this pride does not sound the same as it did the first time it was reported. There is no longer the need to look around the room and see how everyone is responding. There is beginning comprehension as to how feelings affect behavior. The consequences of behavior have consciously become more painful.

Hostile accusations directed at each other and focused on behavior or physical characteristics are less frequent. If it happens, the attacking group member is no longer admired but often receives censure. When one child becomes upset, the group shares the upset. Their caring is usually shown in primitive attempts to console or comfort. Calls of "crybaby" are rarely heard. The group feels some of each child's hurt, perhaps more as it relates to themselves rather than as it does to the upset child. The group turns to the therapist, watching how he or she physically and verbally comforts the upset child. Noting the effect this has on the child, they learn a new way to handle upsets, with empathy and compassion.

The children are beginning to realize that alternatives of behavior exist and can be chosen. The observing ego that has been developing in previous stages is now being used. Instead of simply repeating old cycles, they are getting different responses, and this feedback helps them to control their behavior. Time out is needed infrequently, but when it is needed, good use is made of the time given to the child to help regain self-control. Seldom does a child need to be forcefully removed from the room or need physical controlling; when this does happen, it is more upsetting to the group than previously. The therapist should discuss this situation with the group and expect the children to be angry with him. Part of this anger may arise from the feeling that the therapist may have been unfair to a group member, but the bulk of it relates to each child's own anxiety that he too might need to be removed or leave the group that is so important to him. In spite of criticism and group pressure, the therapist often attempts an explanation even if he feels no one is listening.

The children are growing stronger in their feelings for each other. The child who has previously perceived his problems with peers as outside himself has only minimally used the group but now is beginning to see that the problem may be inside himself.

This needs to be interpreted and supported. The therapist does everything in his power to help laggards reach this point.

The children begin actually to hear each other, comfortably sharing stories and feelings. They now can more actively support each other with statements such as "I know what you mean, my mom's the same way" and "What a drag that must be." The children are reaching out to each other in the form of a playful punch, an arm around the shoulder, or a stroke on the head. If the therapist and children stopped to think about it, it is apparent that a change has taken place. A feeling of groupness and cohesiveness is present. "You're my friends; I never had any before."

Children and therapist eagerly anticipate the group. Everyone feels close, and the atmosphere is quiet, warm, and caring. Children arrive early and have difficulty leaving when the sessions end. The therapist too finds himself ready for the group earlier than he was previously. The children hurry to enter the group room, sitting down immediately and expectantly. If someone is late, the group demands an explanation as he enters. He is forgiven if he has a good excuse. Tardiness of the therapist will be met with anger, and the children will demand that he make amends.

Discussion is intense and group-focused. Even confrontations are done in a supportive manner, rarely provoking fights or angry feelings. The children deal with issues and respond appropriately. The therapist rarely initiates group interaction; he may have to force himself to be quiet. Problems brought by each child become group problems. No one is alone and everyone is aware of this. Empathy, suggestions, and interpretation flow freely from child to child. Subgroups are less rigid and are used for the benefit of group process.

In most groups affection is now openly shared. The therapist's words and actions have demonstrated his views about physical affection. If he has been demonstrative throughout the group life, the children will follow his example. The children will touch each other, offer tissues, or shake hands and may actually hug each other. Children who are not as comfortable with physical contact may bring food for the entire group, or their favorite game, symbolically sharing of themselves.

Play is cooperative and activities are problem-focused. The children may avoid activities and spend the entire session in discussion. When the therapist moves from the discussion before the children are ready, the group forces him back to the issue. Anger flares when he tries to make light of a situation. An interruption is viewed very negatively now. Group pressure is operating at its height, and it may be used to control a group member. It does not take Jimmy long to realize no one appreciates his imitating a dog while the group is trying to work. Jimmy is told to "stop it!" and amazingly he stops. The group has taken over responsibility for control, and any member disagreeing is brought to terms immediately by the group.

Anger may flare, but it is more often over appropriate issues and is marked by an undercurrent of warmth and caring. With increased group sophistication the children may be able to tell each other about it. If they cannot discuss this anger, it must be worked out physically; the children might suggest they Indian-wrestle. Usually not hostile or attacking, the anger more frequently arises out a child's feeling of being hurt or slighted, not by who won the last game or whose cookie was the largest but by the notion that their feelings are not being taken seriously. The children may even get angry at the therapist, if they feel he or she is being unfair or too hard on one child. It is anger more easily resolved, with each taking more responsibility for his or her part in it.

There are more frequent quiet times, not due to anxiety but rather out of respect for the child who is talking, crying, or hurting. The group intuitively knows that sometimes the best way to help is to be quietly with one. Although there is a wish to go on sharing forever, this intensity cannot be maintained.

Group sessions are still eagerly sought and hung onto. The children and therapist are interested in each other. The content of discussion moves almost imperceptibly from a group back to an individual focus. Sharing, practice, and reinforcement are still going on, about everyday incidents and happenings. Awareness is increasing regarding feelings, changes, and ability to handle what could not be handled before. The children like themselves and how they are alike and different from the other group members. They feel great inside. Most things are seen in this positive light, confidence is building, and the children are beginning to feel anxious to see if they can function as well independently. Time and practice provide satisfaction, reassurance, and confidence in these changes. Great joy fills the child's world. Nothing can stop him now.

DYNAMIC DESCRIPTION

The *cohesion stage* is a time of intense psychological closeness. Earlier stages have set the groundwork by establishing basic trust, labeling feelings, and lessening anxiety. Although not exactly sure what to expect, the child and group already feel relief and closer, having shared and survived the anxiety stage. The goals for stage IV are to accomplish individual and group problem solving; to work through original referral problems; and to reap the maximum benefit from group identification, cohesion, and differentiation.

With further analysis three phases become apparent. Phase one begins with the reintroduction of an individual child's problem. The therapist actively prepares the child and group for the process of problem solving and change. Individual commitments are made. Individual problems become as much a part of group focus as group problems. Phase two finds the group experiencing and living through the intense groupness characterized as warm, caring, and cooperative. Group commitments are made and discussion and sharing pervades each session. As phase three begins, the group is a functioning unit, practicing and reinforcing individual and group gains. Members are differentiated, and group identification and internalization are well in process.

The Child

The first phase opens with "I think you're able to help me. I'm now willing to look at myself." The child has stayed in the group because there was a promise of something better for him. Moving into this process slowly and cautiously because he is committed to and wants to work on changing, he begins to look at his own behavior. For one child the realization that his behavior and method of relating has consequences is a strong signal that he is preparing himself to do something about this behavior. For another it is the quiet admission that the whole world is not against him. For the child who believes he is totally bad, it is the beginning feeling that there is hope; someone does like and care about him and maybe others will too. The therapist's understanding and reinforcement of the child's positive behavior have given the child proof that things can be better.

With each child's commitment to look within himself, his anxiety changes. Remaining intense, it is no longer a vague, overwhelming feeling that something is terribly wrong. He is able to identify some of his own problems, and to hear, perhaps for the first time, what the therapist and other children are telling him. Denial has a different flavor to it and is not accompanied by wild acting-out behavior but rather by a pout followed by quiet and thoughtful demeanor. The sometimes feeble attempts to talk about his problems have helped him realize his problems are very important to him. Nothing else seems as important to him now as he feels the pain. It is the only thing the child can feel, touch, hear, and see. The feelings sometimes become so intense that he has to have help with them.

Each child's pain has many origins and individualized meanings. It may be the realization that his not getting along with other children may be a result of his own behavior, that he is not just the "innocent victim." It may be believing that his father left home because he was a bad child. It may be learning and understanding that he might still be lovable even though his biological parents gave him up for adoption. Perhaps it is the realization that his mother is too overwhelmed by her own problems to care for him adequately; rather than believing he is causing his mother's problems. It might be one of the thousands of problems that emotionally disturbed children must resolve in their psychotherapeutic process.

The commitment the child makes in phase one is an individual one to change himself, done in the presence of and made to the therapist and group. The therapist is watchful that these changes are realistic and possible to attain. They can be in the areas of openness and sharing of feelings, changes in attitudes, and accepting alternative behavior responses. A latency-age child may choose to list verbally what he would like to change about himself, or he and the therapist may choose to write these down, signing them, and distributing copies to the child, therapist, group, and parents. Frequently just the process of identifying and focusing on specific problems is organizing and motivating enough to begin real problem solving and change. Nonverbal agreements are sufficient in younger, less disturbed, and less acting-out children, who are participating in more play or activity-oriented therapy than verbal, discussion-oriented therapy.

As phase two begins, each child has a real and vital place in the group, important both to the therapist and other members. The group is very important to him and he feels very committed to it. It is a place where he can talk, be heard and understood, and where his hurt is made less. He no longer needs to act out to keep from acknowledging other children's problems. He allows them to talk because he likes them and feels his problems may be similar and that he can learn from them. His anxiety has been lessened by talking about his feelings and getting some relief. He begins to understand on some level how talking and sharing help. Initially the child had looked mostly to the therapist, but he has learned that the other children have helpful ideas and say things to show they understand too. Some of them have exactly the same problems—their mother is always yelling at them, or they are not allowed back in school either. The child listens intently to what other children have to say; it is important to him that they try to be honest and open. Each child is extremely vulnerable. They sense this in each other and become protective to avoid hurting each other.

The child's functioning is beginning to improve inside the group. With this awareness he begins to feel more intact and relates his changes to the group, frequently believing that without the group he would have been the same or perhaps worse. He has practiced appropriate behaviors in the group, and they do work. He attributes these changes to the group and thinks if it were to go on forever his functioning would certainly improve. He does not understand how he could possibly live without the group and may even wish the therapist could be his parent and each member a brother or sister. He arrives earlier each session and has difficulty leaving the room when the session is over.

The child's commitment to the group is total. He understands how children can and do help each other. Able to help and make someone else feel better, he learns he does have something to give. These children who only a few weeks ago were poking him, teasing him, and calling him names, do understand him and do listen to him. This week Johnny put his arm on his shoulder and Jerry shook his hand. Maybe he is still being poked, but the poke now has an affectionate touch to it. He is liked by the others. They have made their commitment to group goals and changes and are working on these together. The motivating factor for the child now is for some relief from the pain that remains and the proven promise that things can be better. His observing ego has been watching for some time. He is dropping old defenses and behaviors and developing new, more acceptable ones. He tries these first in the group. These changes become more consistent as the child finds the other group members respond to him more positively. The child is in the process of internalizing the therapist and group members and is beginning a solid group identification.

Children with very disturbed parents may have accepted the fact that their parents are disturbed and different. They are learning that they are separate from them and that they can improve their own functioning. They also may be learning that their parents are not changing concurrently and that sometimes things are worse for them now that they have changed through treatment. They feel the group gives them strength to cope with their home environment. In order for the children to have accomplished this separation from their parents, they have substituted a symbiotic-type relationship with the therapist and group, which gradually dissolves as they begin their steps of improved functioning within and outside the group. They return as needed to the group for necessary nurturance and support. New relationships with friends or new dimensions in relationships with family and friends are beginning to gain in importance. They, along with the children from less disturbed or destructive home environments, slowly begin to feel that the changes they have made are a part of them, not only as group members but as individuals.

The process of internalizing the group and therapist is solidifying. The child may surprise himself to hear words and expressions the therapist has used come out of his own mouth, while another child has little awareness that his movements resemble those of the therapist. Another child stops to think before he responds to some provocation, remembering what had transpired in the past when the therapist and/or group used to intervene to get him to observe what had happened. Improvement begins to take place outside the group. It may take reporting an incident to the group for the child to realize how much better he is handling situations. With time, practice, and positive reinforcement, these new ways of handling himself become stronger, more automatic, and less conscious. Internalization is difficult to assess externally and varies according to the age of the child, stage of object relations, and degree of pathology.

The second phase of stage IV begins as the child feels more intact individually, differentiated from the rest of the group. Each child is able to look at himself, realistically evaluating the ways he has changed. In addition to internalized control, he has some awareness of what he cannot control. The child from an exceptionally bad environment, or the physically handicapped child, has begun this acceptance and is learning to compensate. He has gained strength and insight from the therapist and other group members. He is taking these gains with him. He feels great inside, different from, yet a part of, the group. Although the group is still extemely important, the investment and energy required is different. It functions almost on its own, to be there as it's needed. It is no longer the sole occupant of the children's thoughts and energies.

The child's energies and commitments begin to be directed toward the outside world, where he is beginning to be convinced he can function independently. He knows he is changed, feels okay inside, and is anxious to continue his growth outside the group. Anticipation and great joy fill his world. While this "high" will not last forever, the child enjoys it immensely now.

The Therapist

The therapist enters stage IV with great relief. Finally he is beginning to see the fruits of his labors. He lived through stage III but does not believe he could ever do it again. He finds it hard to believe that these are the same children who 3 weeks ago had him convinced that he was in the wrong field. Now his attitude has changed to believing once again he can work with groups of children and even enjoy them! He no longer has to raise his voice and feel like a policeman spending his entire time setting limits. The children respond when asked and, amazingly enough, are beginning to set limits for one another. The therapist finds that his attempts at affection and positive reinforcement are no longer rebuffed. Children who previously screamed "Don't touch me" are now asking for a pat on the back or for their hair to be tousled. The therapist is amazed that these children, who 2 weeks ago denied they had any problems, are now talking openly and honestly about things that upset them, are beginning to look at themselves, and are taking more responsibility for their behavior. This is very rewarding for the therapist. He realizes that he must have done something right, but it can also feel like an awesome responsibility. The novice therapist begins to wonder how he will handle all of these gruesome stories. "Eric keeps bringing up his father, how is Jimmy going to handle this since his father died last year?"

How the therapist deals with the material an individual child brings up is crucial for the group and depends a great deal on his theoretical orientation. Of prime importance in this model is that both individual and group foci exist side by side. Phase one finds the therapist reiterating and clarifying individual and group goals, looking for children ready to make individual commitments. The first child daring to remention his problem is helped by gentle questioning to enhance clarification and understanding. The therapist encourages group members to participate in this process and to relate it to their own feelings and experiences. His activity level has increased as he encourages hesitant children to speak, asks for group validation of feelings and experiences, and interprets behaviors as relating to feelings. These individual commitments usually precede group ones.

The therapist's influence over the expression and solution of problems is of the utmost during this stage. If he becomes overwhelmed by a problem or an individual child's pain, the child and group will become immobilized. Unless temporary, this condition can result in a depressed group or blocked group that cannot enter into the most intimate phase of the group's life. Each child's pain is so intense in phase one that the therapist, especially the novice, literally can feel his body ache for each child. This triggers feelings of wanting to rescue the child, take him home, or at least take his pain away. The therapist soon realizes he cannot make it his own, allow it to overwhelm him, or falsely reassure the child. He deals with his countertransference issues, hoping to demonstrate to the child and group that he does not feel as helpless, hopeless, and immobilized as the child does.

The therapist has learned to offer support, understanding, and advice while at the same time demonstrating that pain can be a motivating, mobilizing factor. He also has learned that some children need to be stopped from exposing too much to the group before he or they are ready to handle it, or that a psychotic child needs controlling of his bizarre verbiage. This may be structured by allowing discussion of one problem at a time or by gently but firmly silencing the child. Therapeutic skill is tested here much the same as in individual treatment except for the added dynamics of a therapy group. It is a constant process of understanding words and behaviors and interpreting them accurately and compassionately to the child and the entire group. The therapist is very busy with his job of helping the children to integrate cognitively and emotionally their life experiences as they relate to their behaviors. He now can relish doing "what a therapist is supposed to be doing in therapy."

Most of what the therapist says is heard and not denied or defended against in phase three. Children also are hearing each other. They have begun to take over functions of the therapist in an identification with him. The therapist feels pleasure and sometimes amusement as he hears the children using the same language and interpretations, spoken with meaning as if they were the children's own words. The therapist is filled with warm feelings for the group, looks forward to group meetings, and hates to see them end. He feels successful and understands the marvels of group process. He is known to brag about how great group therapy can be.

There are only two uncomfortable adjustments during the second phase for the therapist to contend with. Close, intense sessions often are followed by sessions where little seems to be accomplished and there is much vacillation. Experience shows that some distance is needed to integrate, requiring the children to maintain a plateau or status quo before returning to a cohesive group. The other adjustment is dealing with no longer being *the* central person in the group. He must deal with his feelings of being excluded and not being as powerful and important. As the group begins taking over for itself, the therapist must allow this, no longer being as active in facilitating and interpreting so that the children learn to differentiate and become independent.

The therapist realizes that the goals of the group have largely been accomplished and stage IV is coming to an end. He almost hates the thought of it, as the group is running so smoothly now. The therapist knows the gains are strong and internalized and that he and the group have served their purpose. Yet the therapist, like the children is ambivalent. While he helps the child with his mixed feelings by reinforcing the changes, he also deals with his own. Although there are some goals left unaccomplished, he realizes the children are ready to enter stage V.

The Group

This stage is a period of calm after the storm. The group is less physically active, but is a group. The first positive group feeling was participating in asserting controls and sharing in the relief of having completed the anxiety stage. If a group member was lost at the end of that stage, now the group is able to mourn its loss. During phase one the therapist is still looked to as the major authority and nurturing figure. The child is preoccupied with himself and his problems and is not aware if this has an impact on or is shared by other group members. As individual goals and commitments are redefined, the therapist facilitates some of these becoming group goals.

Group goals set in stages I and II are restated, clarified, dropped, or modified in phase two. An original goal, that the children talk about feelings instead of acting them out, is still agreed on, but different expectations may be set for different members. One may need a label for his feeling before he can talk about it, while another may need assistance separating his feelings from those of other members. A commitment has been made to the group by each child: to allow the other group members to work on their problems and to actively help and support them while working on his own. Group commitment differs from individual commitment in that group wishes and goals are equal to or take priority over individual ones. The group begins to jell as these group commitments and contracts are made.

Fairness and equality are prominent in the group. In stage III the therapist had to be fair because each child was frightened that the others might get more than he would. They have made significant changes in the area of sibling rivalry by this time, and the benefits are seen in phase two. The children are secure that they all have an equally special place with the therapist. Even though the children feel equal, differing roles are present. The child who earlier set himself up as a scapegoat may still be scapegoated but with an understanding of why he does it and what he gets out of it. He and the group are aware of their respective roles, point them out, and often laugh about them. It is no longer a destructive attack, but representative of their problems in life and their newly learned acceptance and understanding. Dyads and subgroups are no longer separate from the group but are nuclei around which closeness is expressed. Disagreements and differences are expressed comfortably and are not disruptive to the group's well-being.

Closeness expressed in this stage is both physical and emotional. The children pull their chairs together. The therapist is included, no longer standing apart as the most important group member. The give and take of the children is significant, and they respond openly and warmly. Group cohesion and identification contribute to the group's feeling of confidence and power. Outside attacks, if any, are warded off and viciously fought against. The group entity exists with strong positive valences, made possible as a result of the processes of internalization and group identification.

Phase three begins slowly as the group revels in its intimacy. Members' accomplishments and achievements click off as they expand their relationships. There develops a realization that the group's goals have been achieved and its members have changed. Sometimes slowly, sometimes quickly, the group looks again at its goals. Vacillation between knowing and fearing that the group really has accomplished its purposes is present.

The Parents

Parents rarely complain during this stage and may wonder why their child is still in treatment. Most parents are thrilled with the improvement and take pleasure in the gains. Although some parents may wish their child had improved more quickly, they are still proud. They may start noticing symptoms in another child and suggest to the therapist that Eric's brother now needs help.

The Agency

The agency is seldom heard from in stage IV except for a remark that individual children or the group seem better, calmer. If a child is sent out of the group room, he usually can be counted on to stay where he is put and to be in fairly good control of himself. The therapist may hear from the receptionist and from his colleagues that the group is not disrupting them anymore. Other therapists, in a joking manner, will ask the group therapist, "What did you do, crack the whip?"

The group therapist may now brag about how well his group is doing. To his friends he will say that the group is really into it and may get suggestions on how to handle certain issues. The peace and satisfaction the group therapist feels will permeate to the rest of the agency.

Handling Content and Feelings

Stage IV finds the child, group, and therapist experiencing intense feelings of both psychic pain and closeness. Together, they are called on to handle these difficult feelings, sometimes requiring great empathy, strength, and therapeutic expertise.

The anxiety manifest in this stage is more focused and contained and is more individually related to a child's conflictual issues. As the child is ready, the therapist encourages him to talk about his own anxiety and pain, letting him know that he is there to help and support. When necessary, this encouragement includes labeling for the child what if feels like when upset and how the child uses various behaviors to protect himself from his pain. The therapist uses his clinical skills in assessing the child's, the group's, and his own reaction to the latent content and underlying anxiety in the child's message and behavior, to gain more information regarding the source of the anxiety.

Children vary greatly in how much they can and should open up. Some very disturbed children do not have enough ego boundaries to help keep from "spilling all." Revealing too much is not helpful to these children or to the group, as it only causes increased anxiety. These children need careful structuring and containment of their verbal content. Although it rarely occurs, if a child reveals too much, "falling apart" during the group, it is most helpful for the child and group if the reconstruction can be done during the same group session, even if it means a longer meeting time.

Some children dealing with difficult issues become anxious and have difficulty feeling the presence and support of the therapist without physical touching. Frequently all that is needed to calm down the child and enable him to work on resolving an issue is for the therapist to put his hand on the child's arm, knee, or back to reassure him of the therapist's presence and caring. The therapist should acknowledge to the child that even though he knows how difficult it is for him to talk about such things, he is happy and proud that he is gradually able to.

Phase two brings with it a change in the therapist's typical role of facilitator, clarifier, teacher, interpretor, and authority figure. As each member reaches equanimity and group cohesion is at its height, the therapist adjusts to a temporary, more passive experiencing position. Group members deal with him much as they do any of their peer group members. They are now identified with him, having incorporated his caring, attitudes, and techniques. They now wish to know more about him as a person and about his relationships, as their central issue is now dealing with relationships. They also are doing this with one another. This is one of their last steps in the process of identification. The content of their exploration usually surrounds how the therapist's spends his time, personally and professionally. Similarly, they want to know what their peers do too. In this necessary process of identification they are open and available for taking in as much as possible from therapist and all group members in this safe practice arena. Each session brings with it concrete examples of solid and stable growth inside the group.

Phase three is in process as each makes strides to expand and continue this growth outside the group, taking with him all of his accomplishments and new sense of self. This individual sense of self has been bolstered by all of the growth that has been reinforced through the process of group identification. A process of differentiation from the group is beginning. The therapist recognizes, supports, and appreciates the child's discussion of how he is different and separate from the group and the other members. The therapist can step back and revel in the mysteries and wonders of the internal processes of identification and differentiation.

Co-Therapists

The co-therapy relationship is a smoother functioning unit; each complements the other, picking up where the other ends or with what the other misses. The group has reached this point in the group life partially as a result of the co-therapist team. The children have observed and experienced how they talk, work, and relate to one another.

By the end of phase one, disagreements over the meaning or interpretation of behavior were discussed openly in front of the children, thus allowing the children to see two sides of a problem and demonstrating that adults can reach resolutions, not necessarily agreements, without yelling and screaming. Sometimes the group's opinion had been sought. The co-therapists are a team, experiencing the same intense closeness the children are, with themselves and the group. They are openly available as models of identification.

The children are now curious about the relationship between therapists and will question it. The children, observing closeness in the co-therapy relationship, are confused about the nature and meaning of close adult relationships. If the therapists are of opposite sexes, the children will frequently ask if they are in love or having sexual intercourse. If they are the same sex, the children will want to know if they are friends and do things together. They want to know if they get together and discuss the children and group. Statements that men and women can be friends and care about each other without having sexual relationships may be helpful. Co-therapy during stage IV can be a rewarding, fulfilling experience, enabling staff to become close to each other and to know each other in a way that might otherwise have been impossible.

Confidentiality

Whatever the relationship between the parents and therapist, the child must understand that the therapist and group belong to him, not his parents. The group also is informed of their responsibility regarding confidential information—that they not mention names when relating incidents nor pass on information to friends or family. If this message of confidentiality is not repeated or clearly understood by the group, they may not be able to reveal intimate and disturbing feelings and information.

Occasionally parents will try to elicit specific information from the therapist. "What did Johnny say? Did he tell you about the fight in school?" If the child wishes to discuss it with his parents, it is the child's decision. Parents are best advised to give their child openings to talk to them if he wishes to do so, but they should not push the issue.

In situations where the child has done something the therapist judges dangerous, the therapist must deal with his doubts about breaking his confidentiality pledge. These situations are rare and should be considered individually. After it is clear that the child is not exaggerating or confabulating, the situation is weighed with previous experiences. If the incident is judged sufficiently dangerous, the therapist should tell the child and the group that he feels the child is in danger and that he, the therapist, must talk to the child's parents. The child should be allowed to express his feeling about this and have the opportunity to inform his parents if he wishes.

Absences and Changes in Membership

Absences are even more upsetting in the cohesion stage. Each child is very invested in the group, attached to other members, and will try to attend at all costs. Although absences rarely occur, the group should be encouraged to discuss them thoroughly. If possible, the therapist tries to elicit the children's fantasies about why a member is missing. In that way he or she can reassure them it was not because of something they said or did. Whatever the reason for the child's absence, the therapist should expect the group to miss the member and to react with feelings of sorrow, anger, and denial. This abbreviated mourning also will reflect the child's place and status in the group.

This is the last stage in which members are removed, and this occurs only when a child is destroying the progress of the group. Such children have been closely monitored through stage III and dropped as indicated. Occasionally the therapist has delayed the decision until phase one of stage IV, hoping the child might still change. However, if a child is incapable of individualization by this time, if he has very poor behavioral controls, cannot tolerate change, and actively moves to prevent others' change, he will have to be dismissed from the group. This task is the therapist's, as rarely do children this disturbed remove themselves. Sometimes in fairly well-functioning groups, the other group members help to force the issue. It is best done as rapidly as possible, after being discussed with the child and the remaining group members and having been made clear that it was the therapist's decision. Generally, children no longer fear the same will happen to them, but they still experience a sense of relief. This relief may or may not be accompanied by guilt.

Given the therapist's preference, children are rarely added to close-ended groups during this stage. In a short, time-limited group a child would not be added. If exceptions are made, the group should be carefully prepared, and the new member might spend a few sessions with the therapist. The child should be relatively intact, able to verbalize, and ready to work on his problems. It is helpful if the child has had some therapy previously. The child should be prepared for some anger from the other children and comparison to the old member.

Adding a new child during this stage need not be destructive to the group. Provided they have been allowed to ventilate their mixed feelings prior to his or her arrival, they might help orient the new child to how they function and to what has happened in earlier sessions. The new child should be able to make an adjustment without a great deal of difficulty. Depending on the group, ages, and pathology, the children should be back into this working stage after a few sessions of regression. There will be some testing and hesitancy to deal with their problem in front of the new child until they feel he or she can be trusted. The other children in the group are so invested in the treatment process and are in such pain that it takes more than a new member to stop them at this point.

In an open-ended group, new children constantly enter into this intimate phase. The group soon learns this procedure and, along with the therapist, learns the quickest way to help the new child enter.

Chapter 7

STAGE V: TERMINATION

Charles H. Herndon

EXPERIENTIAL DESCRIPTION

Individual members of the group are comfortable with each other, and group discussion flows easily. There is a strong sense of "groupness," and the therapist is rarely needed for limit setting. Discussions about outside activities and new friends increase. Beginning talk is heard about plans for the future, sometimes with other members of the group. Last week Jason mentioned he was bored with the group because all they did was talk about things they have been doing, and he would rather be playing baseball.

The therapist finds himself muddling over whether he should introduce the fact there are only eight sessions left. By the time he feels ready, two more sessions have passed, and Mark is the one who brings the issue to a head by asking, "How much longer do we go on?" Another therapist, with only five more sessions remaining, may have resolved enough of his or her own feelings to bring up the subject, before a child questions it.

The group's reaction is puzzling. Some members react with surprise—"Oh, no." Others show no apparent reaction. Although one may say, "It's about time!" his behavior demonstrates this is not so. The calm that was present is clearly beginning to crumble. Poignant silences appear, as if a favorite balloon had been broken. The therapist finds himself talking to fill these by enumerating the gains they all have made. He begins to feel himself "grandstanding," calmly trying to lower the anxiety that has crept into and taken over the room. Almost as if to reassure himself, he says, "There is plenty of time left, five sessions, to do what we need to do."

At this point Andy and Mark get into a fight, and Jenny puts her hand over the therapist's mouth. The novice therapist is struck with anxiety. He wonders if the group is really ready to end. The anger and denial confronting him is reminiscent of earlier onslaughts. The group no longer has the feeling of groupness. He feels overwhelmed and wonders if it all has been worth the effort, as achieved gains seem so quickly to disappear. He gently removes Jenny"s hand and tells the group again that it makes him sad but the group is going to end. Some members express their anger by saying they hated "the dumb group" anyway. Limits are rechecked for the trillionth time; as always, the children are looking for caring from the therapist.

Almost immediately after the announcement of the final date, regression is noted both in the group and in individual members. The therapist talks about this with the group. "You don't need that kind of behavior anymore." "I know when I feel sad or like something is being taken away from me, I sometimes act in ways that I know I no longer need or that are not helpful to me." "Leaving is hard, scary, and sad." Sometimes all the therapist is able to fit in is a staccato message, "Cut that out." "No, you don't need to do that." "Stop that." Anxiety and anger trigger quick tempers. "What's happened to the group?"

The group may begin spontaneously to recapitulate earlier events, or the therapist may initiate this process. "Do you remember when Mark hit Andy and they both started screaming?" Laughter follows. "Do you remember that boy who left the group?" Earlier losses may be talked about with a different focus and meaning as the group tries to prepare for separation. This process helps to return the group equilibrium and feeling.

Jason protests, though, with "I still fight with my brother, and my parents still yell at me." Others join him in talking about goals not quite accomplished or expectations unfulfilled. Some of the children comment on their changes but fear they will lose all gains if they do not have the group to support them. The therapist tries to explain how the changes are now inside them, and although it may be harder for them, they will be able to continue their improved functioning. They have "learned skills that will help them do this."

The therapist helps the group begin to evaluate itself by asking members what they have gotten out of the group. Adolescents may be able to evaluate the group and their experiences very accurately. The therapist talks about how each child has progressed. He asks for ideas about future recommendations and discusses what he had in mind for each one. Some children can discuss their plans and seek support and others' opinions. As much as they are able to, together they make plans.

Allison begins to talk more openly about the abuse she suffered earlier in her life. Several children seem to work harder during these last few sessions than they have previously. They seem to want to say everything that is on their minds. Sometimes the fact that the group is ending also makes revealing material less threatening.

During the final sessions some of the group members are able to talk about their sadness at the loss of the group. One child says to the therapist, "I will miss you. You are my best friend." The children may exchange telephone numbers and vow to meet again. There is a fantasy that the group can continue on as it has been. "If you care, how can you let us go?" Some children come earlier and stay later to spend every last minute with the therapist and group. Other children try to avoid the termination by coming late or not at all. The therapist talks about his sadness at the loss of this group and how this group is special and different from all others.

Although some groups are not functioning very cohesively, a child or the therapist may suggest a closing party, a kind of "graduation party." The therapist may wish to give it, symbolically wishing to give more of himself, or a group may wish to share in the plans and preparations. Most enjoy the celebration and are proud of their accomplishments, and it can sometimes help pull together a group that has really pulled apart during the termination stage.

There is discomfort expressed by all during the final session, reminiscent of the opening session. But usually there is more happiness than sadness. As the children begin their good-byes, a child may hug the therapist or shake his hand. The therapist says good-bye to each child and usually sees them out of the group room so as not to feel the pain of an empty room. Some children make a point to say good-bye to everyone in the agency, especially if they are terminating all treatment. As the last child leaves, the therapist may blink back a tear.

Dynamic Description

The goal of this stage is for the children and the group to separate as successfully and as completely as possible while maintaining and utilizing the gains they have made throughout therapy. "Ideally, the termination phase represents a point where the member and/or group have completed their major goals for therapy and begin to move out of the group" (Levine, 1979, p. 77).

The importance of this stage is a somewhat debated issue in the literature. Braaten's (1974/1975) review of group development models revealed that only 5 out of 14 had termination stages. Slavson and Schiffer (1975) do not deal with a group-as-a-whole terminating. They suggest termination be handled by the parents and make only a few references to it in their entire volume. They terminate children as they are ready and stop a group at the end of a school year, shifting those not ready to "transitional groups." On the other hand, Garland, Jones, and Kolodny (1976) stress that "when we fail to recognize the impact that the group experience and its attendant relationships have on individuals, we tend to minimize and deny feelings of loss that the members and we ourselves have when it is time to part" (p. 64).

What earmarks the beginning of this termination process also differs in the literature. Rose (1972) introduces the fact of termination during the first group session and feels it should become a regular item on the agenda for at least 2 months before the end (p. 187). Levine (1979) views the termination phase as beginning with the "final separation crisis," which is initiated "by the therapist's or member's recognizing that the end is in sight" (pp. 241-242).

The authors view termination as an important stage that begins prior to the first statement by the therapist or question by a member regarding the group's end. Either, and more often both, the group members or the therapist had been aware that the group's end was imminent but had been denying and avoiding the fact because of the wish to continue the cohesive group feelings so prominent during stage IV. The statement of termination evokes differing but equally strong separation reactions and coping devices. These emotional reactions contain denial, anger, regression, hostility, acting out, grief, relief, joy, and pride. Various group members may express these simultaneously, in tandem, or in juxtaposition. All may be evident in flashes during one session or may cluster more sequentially in different sessions.

Regardless of the length of the group, a minimum of three sessions is necessary for termination. A group that has met for 9 months more than once a week may need six to eight sessions to terminate. Groups of hospitalized children may need only three group sessions to terminate group therapy, as they will be dealing with termination throughout their days. If the termination is too long, the group may suffer dropouts; if it is too short, the therapist may have visitors for weeks after the last session.

On closer examination the termination stage divides into three conceptual phases. During phase one the group has begun to introduce and discuss happenings outside the group. The therapist begins in earnest his or her evaluation of the group and the individuals in it. The formal statement of the termination date initiates phase two. This precipitates anxiety and a separation crisis. Separation reactions and coping devices are the processes in evidence during phases two and three. Their expression is not the same in all groups and is very dependent on earlier group experiences and sequence in handling emotional issues in earlier stages. This is especially true of the way a group may have progressed through stage II and its characteristic

mode of dealing with crises, especially previous separation crises, which may have arisen around dropouts or losses. Garland
et al. (1976) also have observed this phenomena of an unorderly
progression relating to separation.

The third phase is a time of recapitulation, reminiscing, and
reviewing that is done by the entire group. Resharing of the
group's previous feelings and experiences as it passed through
stages I through IV, helps consolidate growth. There are many
memories to recapture. The children have increased feelings of
self-esteem and have been successful in making and keeping
friendships, increasing their skills and levels of mastery. This internalization of the group and therapist, and this acquisition of
new ego strengths and functioning, has been gradually taking
place throughout the entire group life. Termination offers each
member a chance to further solidify this process and to let go of
one another. The manner in which the child is able to accomplish this greatly affects the total success of his or her group
treatment. The group has progressed from desperate individuals to combatants to cohesive buddies to integrated, individuated
beings.

Termination in children's and adolescent groups offers
golden opportunities to work on developmental tasks and separation issues. Separation-individuation is often faulty or incomplete and may be an underlying reason for referral. Sometimes a
child's behavior or personality disorder is found to be wholly or
in part caused by loss that has not been adaptively coped with.
The large numbers of children seen in clinics with divorce, de-
sertion, and death in their case histories tends to attest to this.
Adolescence has as one of its main tasks the separation from
parents. Careful consideration and planning is needed to provide an atmosphere to help the child and the group rework
some earlier losses while also dealing with the group's end. The
process of separation brings up these earlier losses. The fact that
these current and earlier separation phenomena occur and are
shared in the group adds the supportive experience that the
child is not alone with his losses and that others have them too.
Successful experience with separation helps the child in his development. Each success adds a progressive step from "diffuse"
to "differentiation" to "integration" (Pine, 1971).

The Child

During phase one topics of conversation, questions, and feelings about *outside* things begin appearing. At first these are sporadic and often not paid much attention to, but as they gain in importance and meaning to the child, they begin to be more intently listened to by therapist and group. More information and support for their importance is given, laying the groundwork for termination. Outside increasingly becomes a part of the member's experience in the group. New friends, peer groups, conflicting time schedules, and changes at home make their appearance. The therapist interprets why these things are becoming more important, always reconfirming the caring and support. Originally unaware of this subtle shift, each child enjoys it, liking to share his mastery. The recognition and reinforcement the child feels from the group, the therapist, and often his parents and the school help solidify his or her improved ego functioning and integration.

This progressive growth scenario does not always exhibit itself in practice, especially during phase two. Whereas one group of children may enter the termination stage in this manner, another, which all along has had difficulty dealing with losses, may enter it quite differently. The group that had an explosive and difficult anxiety stage will most likely repeat many of these patterns during termination. The number of and diversity of coping devices and defensive reactions to termination are reminiscent of patterns seen in stages II, III, and IV. Ambivalence during termination is seen in a kind of tug of war: wishing to avoid and regress while also wishing to master and move on. At any given moment the stronger pull is seen and expressed systematically in bits and pieces or in flashes and clusters.

It may be the more anxious or put-together child who heralds the beginning of phase two by raising the question "How many more sessions are there?" Even though the therapist may have said during the first session that the group would end when school let out, it now becomes the focal issue. The next session's comments reflect ambivalence and the natural process of separation: "I'm glad this group is ending, so I can play with my friends." "Anyway, we don't have fun anymore in this group."

"Remember the good times and trouble we used to get into?" "What am I going to do when the group ends?" "After summer we can meet again and have a good time." "This group hasn't helped anyway; I still get into trouble." "Let's plan a big bash our last day." "I'm never coming back!" "I never did like coming and talking anyway." "Let's get together and go to the movies." "Maybe I don't need this group anymore; I get along at school and my parents don't bug me."

Children prepare themselves in different ways and in different sequences for functioning without the group. Most children deny feelings of anger and pain. Some will be able to grieve, cry, or express their fears, while others talk about what the group has meant to them. Fond memories are sprinkled with shared chuckling, embarrassment, and bravado. What they share in common is an accepting therapeutic group atmosphere that provides support, caring, and nurturance. Some children, due to the fact that termination is imminent, begin verbalizing in a way not previously shown. One may reveal hidden feelings or experiences; another may integrate and consolidate gains.

The major portion of the therapeutic work during termination is reminiscing, reconfirming in the present, and looking forward to the future. During phase three each child learns that he has changed, now having something new and lasting inside that is just his. The child can easily distinguish himself from the problems and feelings of the others, making his boundaries stronger and clearer.

During the group separation process the child continues internalizing and strengthening gains he has made. Even though a child may be acutely aware of his identification with and dependence on the group, he still believes he has changed. This comprehension aids the child and enables him to say good-bye without overwhelming loss or devastation. This is a highly individualized process dependent on the child's psychic structure and previous separation-individuation experiences. The child may additionally benefit from seeing other children cope with their losses in different ways. For the child for whom separation has been experienced as a loss of a part of himself, observation of others not fragmenting may be beneficial.

There are children who cannot cope with the termination

and take flight, not returning to sessions. Attempts to get them back are generally unsuccessful. The group may experience this as a rejection and utilize it to project their own feelings of anger and loss. Focusing on how others deal with their good-byes can help the remaining children deal with their own feelings of loss.

Not all groups are able to discuss termination in helpful, rational ways and can simply be described as chaotic and fragmentary. The therapist tries to lessen anxiety by returning to structured activities and trying to rebuild cohesion. He may organize an ending party. The group goal becomes to remain together through the final session.

The Therapist

The therapist enters stage V as a member of the group. He monitors, guides, listens, and interprets only as necessary. Much of the group material arising spontaneously is handled by the group itself. He listens intently to the increase in discussion of activities outside of the group. His stance has changed regarding the expression of this material. In previous sessions, when he felt it was defensive, he might have limited the group discussion to what occurred within the group. By phase one if outside material does not come up spontaneously; the therapist encourages it. With children undergoing their first successful group experience, he must increase the attractiveness of outside groups. Rose (1972) explains how to help accomplish this: increase outside friendships, increase attractiveness of outside activities, and decrease the attractiveness of the therapist. (p. 188).

Early in phase one, while the group is still functioning smoothly, the therapist is advised to evaluate each member's and the group's functioning. This work is crucial now in order to have a realistic assessment prior to the first announcement of termination. The presenting complaint, the change in the individual child, and his or her developmental level are all considered in relationship to the child's environment. The group's cohesiveness, ability to allow differentiation, and support of emotional growth are reviewed: "Will this group be able to continue its empathetic bond during the process of separation and allow both sides of the ambivalence to be expressed?" "How is the separation process likely to proceed for these individuals and group?"

Phase two begins as the therapist gently expresses what has been covertly felt but consistently avoided: "Yes, the group will end in six sessions, but we have plenty of time left to do what we need to." The therapist then must be prepared for an onslaught of responses.

Some respond with anger or regress and return to behaviors exhibited in stage III. The therapist handles this increased anxiety reassuringly. This is easier as the lines of communication and trust are firmly established. He remains consistent in his focus and caring. "The rules remain the same." "No, you don't need to do that." "I know you are angry and that's okay." "I feel sad too." "I know you don't want the group to end, but you will be able to function without me and the group." Others react as if nothing has been said. The therapist repeats himself. "If avoidance is extreme . . . the therapist must confront the group with their behavior" (Yalom, 1970, p. 281). He has had to return to a more active, directive role, interpreting as indicated the connections with earlier losses. Little or no time is left to enjoy the feeling of being a group member or of being able to assess accurately the progress of the group or individuals. The therapist who did not evaluate in phase one finds himself almost hopelessly immersed in the process. He or she experiences doubts about individual and group growth.

Group reminiscing, recapitulation, and evaluation occur during phase three. Although not all groups are equally able to experience this process, as they are able they remember what it used to be like. Previously enjoyable and traumatic events invade with a feeling of shared amusement and accomplishment. Together they may be able to look at the group's and each member's present level of ability, strength, and growth. The therapist must buttress recently learned behavior to help integrate and consolidate gains. Expectations for the future are shared. Further recommendations and plans are discussed in the group as appropriate and as time allows. Some may be done in individual conferences. The separation process is assisted by the therapist's sharing each child's and the group's special meaning.

Each therapist handles termination in his or her characteristic manner, but there is a similar process. Some fail to recognize that the group is ready for and may already have begun termination. Perhaps this avoidance is due to a need to prolong the fantasy that the group will go on meeting everyone's needs forever or to avoid the children's anger. It is common for a therapist to focus almost exclusively on getting the group to deal with their termination issues, while denying or ignoring his own. Some, who are more in touch with their feelings, grieve first; others get angry. Some withdraw, separating emotionally from the group.

The authors of this book agree with Levine (1979) and Yalom (1970) about the importance of looking at the therapist's own feelings about the termination process, including difficult self-awareness and countertransference issues. "Saying goodbye to some patients is saying goodbye to a part of ourselves" (Yalom, 1970, p. 280). This is especially true with children, which the authors highlight by adding a final stage, *closure*. The therapist's "ideal parent" role, protective fantasies, and realistic concern about the child's welfare and environment all surface during the process of letting go of children.

The Group

The group begins stage V functioning well and feeling a strong sense of groupness. There is a comfortable predictability in group interactions, and the members rather easily discuss one another's feelings and problems. There is confidence in themselves and their decisions and a substantial change can be noted.

Manner of progression through the termination stage varies greatly and is colored by experiences in stages II, III, and IV. The sessions immediately following the statement of termination often are chaotic, but the anxiety is usually not as intense, nor does it last as long. The therapist focuses on group discussion of separation issues, evaluations, and recommendations. Group pressure may be exerted to keep behavior in line and to keep a member coming, but usually not with quite the same degree of tolerance and empathy as exibited during the cohesive stage. Prior group events, happy and traumatic, will be relived during termination. Any losses of a member or a therapist will be reexperienced, focusing on separation issues.

The Parents

As soon as the termination statement is made in the group, the therapist can begin contacting the parents. Sometimes a parents' group meeting is scheduled to review the group's progress. The agenda will be a review of accomplishments in the group and what to expect during the separation process. Individual appointments may follow for private discussion and to convey recommendations.

The parent-therapist contact and relationship has been consistent and must also have its closure. Parents' feelings, concerns, and questions need to be considered as recommendations are being made. Agencies, names, telephone numbers, dates, and financial matters are covered. Sometimes a letter reviewing the conference is sent to help ensure implementation of recommendation.

The Agency

Although groups vary, the agency in the first phase of stage V is barely aware of a group functioning in the clinic. The children come and go happy and content. Except for illnesses, attendance is perfect. In phase two the agency may not become aware of the regression, anger, and sadness, and complaints are rare.

The agency may experience increased telephone calls to set appointments and search resources, as well as increased paperwork as follow-up plans are made. Treatment staffings, consultations, and referrals also are taking place. Children make their rounds to say special good-byes to those staff important to them. If there is a party, the people acquainted with the children and those having played some role in the group's life are invited.

SPECIAL ISSUES

Terminations, difficult for everyone, are especially so for children, because the major developmental task of childhood is separation and individuation. Children who may be struggling to discover and maintain boundaries in their relationships at home also have had to do so in the group. Now they must separate from the group. The intense familial feelings and identifications inherent in groups had led to conceptualization by Scheidlinger (1974) that the group is like a mother. Trafimow and Pattak (1981) have supported this concept in their work with groups of disturbed children.

Children who have not successfully completed Mahler's (1968) stage's of separation-individuation will have a difficult time with termination because they feel they are losing a part of themselves. Although unable to conceptualize or verbalize this, they may experience a body feeling of being torn apart. This experience produces anxiety and, in some, panic and fragmentation. They may fear that they are not complete and cannot function without the group.

Denial

Denial is frequently the first defense used by children to deal with termination, because the reality of the impending separation may be too painful or anxiety-producing to face. Denial results in a variety of observed behaviors. The group may react as if they never heard the announcement of termination, continuing their play or discussion. They may become "super cohesive" or demonstrate a renewed dependence on the therapist (Johnson, 1974). When the therapist interprets to the group how painful the ending is, how unfair it seems, the children ignore him, tell him to "shut up," or cover their ears or his mouth. A child may "forget," insisting he had never been told anything about the group's ending.

Few therapists use denial about the group's ending, but they avoid introducing it, "forgetting" to announce the date for one or two sessions, delaying the process and not giving adequate time to work through separation. They may deny the group's or children's meaning to themselves, short-circuiting their own grieving by focusing exclusively on the children's grieving. Some therapists who avoid dealing with separation problems of their own unconsciously convey that these feelings are too painful to handle. This results in the group and the therapist being denied the opportunity of working on separation issues.

Regression

Regression is an adaptive defense mechanism used almost universally by children trying to face separation from a group that has become a meaningful part of the their lives. Like most behaviors the kind and extent of the regression needs to be considered. Some believe regression is an essential, integral part of termination.

Garland et al. (1976) identify two types of regression at the group's end. First is "simple disorganized regression," which "is a sliding backward in ability to cope with interpersonal and organizational tasks, usually accompanied by outbursts of anger toward one another and the worker and toward the idea of the club ending" (p. 58). The "regressive fugue" is when members behave in "a manner dramatically reminiscent of earlier developmental stages. This condition . . . reflects a desire to 'begin all over again' and involves a phantasy-like detachment from the here and now of the group" (pp. 58–59).

Regression occurs both with the group and within the children. The group most often regresses to earlier forms of behavior exhibited during stages II and III. The therapist will interpret this, helping the group verbalize and begin the process of reminiscing. Earlier behaviors are recognizable, but often, as a result of the intervening internal changes and increased ego functioning, the quality in individual children is less primitive and pathological. The regression sometimes surprises and frightens the children, parents, and even the therapist. The therapist interprets in light of the previous therapeutic work and the separation process.

Anger

Anger may precede, follow, be mingled with, or used in the service of denial, regression, and grief. It frequently first appears when termination is mentioned and the final date set. It is expressed toward the therapist, the group, the agency, and toward other group members in varying degrees. Anger is often expressed toward absent members. However, regardless of the initial and apparent direction in which the anger is focused, it is always focused at some level on the therapist who is ending this wonderful experience.

Anger at termination is normal. The therapist accepts it and interprets it to the child and group, also expressing his own anger. When anger's expression is prohibited, it is often inappropriately expressed or displaced toward other group members, clinic, or property. When anger is not expressed, interpersonal conflicts in the group increase (Levine, 1967). When the expression of the anger becomes rage, the therapist employs techniques for control found useful during earlier stages. Anger also is used to test again if the rules are still the same and if the therapist understands that the grief has to be warded off. The child wants to know if rejection and termination are synonymous. Some children may be able to verbalize comfortably their anger at termination and are proud of this achievement. They have been taught to express appropriately all of their mixed feelings, making the shift from action to talking.

Grief

Grief, or profound sadness, occurs in addition to denial, regression, and anger. It is hesitant at first, briefly stated, then often denied or rebuffed. As the group's end is acknowledged, a quiet blanket covers the group. Some less defended groups may express their sadness quite openly, with each member stating it plainly, in analogy or metaphor. A well-functioning group may have experienced grief earlier, dealing with it together over the loss of a member or a therapist. It will be brought up as a focal issue again during stage V in a second effort to deal with the pain. In another group a member expresses it while talking about his life, the existential pain of abuse, abandonment, or divorce. Its expression is accompanied almost with a sigh of relief, as it can now be a shared group issue.

Often groups would like to gloss over the feeling and expression of grief. If this is allowed to happen it will be displaced of left unresolved. Only by sharing sadness in the group, by obtaining confirmation, reassurance, and caring from each other will there be comfort felt. The letting go of, resolution of, and healing of grief occurs with this group comforting.

Grief shown during the final session is somewhat different, more ambivalent. It is brief, juxtaposed with happiness, and is more situationally focused. For those denying termination up until the final sessions or for those who have dropped out early, the expression and resolution is most difficult, as it cannot be done in one session and will therefore have to be done alone without feedback and group support. Group fellowship, support, and reality testing is important in working through grief.

Recapitulation

Recapitulation, the process of reenacting, reminiscing, and reviewing, is also a necessary ingredient in the separation process. Garland et al. (1976) also identify two types of recapitulation. The first is "reenactment . . . where earlier modes of interaction, developmental crises, and program events are relived" (p. 60). There may be requests for exact reenactments of previous group activities or merely discussion of significant events in the group's history. "Review" is the second type of recapitulation and "is a more conscious process of reminiscing" (p. 60) about group life and events. Evaluation is seen as being closely tied to reenactment and "reflects a more rationalized and organized experience" (p. 61). Although begun during stage V, review and evaluation often continue beyond the group's end and are therefore highlighted in stage VI.

After a group has shared in their expression of anger and grief, there is a certain freedom to reminisce with both laughter and tears. As glimpses of the "good old group" pass by, the changes are evident. The group is no longer necessary.

Dropouts

According to Yalom (1970) who works with adults, dropouts are rare in this stage. This has not been our experience with children, perhaps because separation issues and tasks are so developmentally current and conflictual. A variety of factors may be at work when members drop out of the group before the announced termination date. One member finds separation too painful, so he or she runs from it. This child may have shown an outburst of temper or a rage attack directed at the therapist, group, or clinic. Another way to recognize this child is that he may cancel sessions for reasons that would not have kept him away during stage IV, or he may just not show. If a member has missed more than a session or two, the therapist may not be able to get him to return. He may have missed so much group work that it will be difficult for him to return or the group to accept him back. The group may be angry and hurt by this behavior, feeling rejected.

The member having separation difficulties should be brought back into the group if possible so that separation can be dealt with as a group issue. If this is not possible, a special meeting should be arranged with the child and his parents. This child needs an explanation of separation issues and an interpretation of his behavior. The therapist points out that these feelings are normal and are felt by all the group members. Sharing good-byes in the group will help free him to begin new relationships.

Another potential dropout is the peripheral group member who has minimally participated and whose pathology greatly differs from the rest of the group. This member may not be ready to terminate or is no longer accepted by the group because he cannot express and manage his feelings at the same level of appropriateness as the group or because he is unable to make similar commitments. It may be important to maintain more disturbed children in the group, so that the others may terminate with them and so as not to be too disruptive to group process.

Yalom (1970) also notes that there are members who make abrupt departures from the group because they find it difficult to express gratitude and positive feelings (p. 279). Although Yalom was referring to adults, this also holds true for some children.

Recommendations

There are numerous avenues open for children following group therapy. The directions chosen will depend on factors such as the goals of the group, the pathology of the children, their ages, and the facilities available in the community. The preschool child who has learned parallel play may now be able to participate in a day nursery program and continue his or her emotional development. The psychotic inpatient may now be able to participate in a day hospital program or special school placement. Another may be able to tolerate a one-to-one relationship and can enter individual psychotherapy. The behavior-disordered child may be able to focus his energy toward scouting, "Y" activities, or sports. Those slow to grow in the group process may have another group experience recommended.

Recommendations are formulated as a result of the therapist's evaluation, and the consultant's and/or treatment staffing's recommendations. Part of the group's termination is talking together about what each may need when the group has ended. Group members are asked their opinions and often have helpful suggestions and knowledge of community resources. Careful thought is given to the child's progress, his comfort and use of the group, and the family's functioning. "Will this child be able to maintain his gains within the family system?" "Is a different school setting or class desirable?"

Whatever the recommendation, it needs to be discussed thoroughly with both the child and his parents in a joint meeting. If the child has been in concurrent therapy, that therapist also may want to be present. Most children, even the very young, can recognize what further help is needed. Some parents have a general understanding by this time of the needs of the child and eagerly await the therapist's recommendations. This is probably one of the most open and gratifying meetings the therapist has with the family, as it is used to discuss gains and recommendations. The child is given approval, sometimes furthering his insight into his accomplishments, which helps him anticipate future expectations. This eliminates some of the pain of separation and starts the joyful expectations that make termination also a happy experience. It also helps reestablish a supportive, empathetic relationship between the child and his parents. Contact should continue to assure that recommendations are implemented. The more complicated they are and the more disturbed the parents, the more frequent the contact.

REFERENCES

Braaten, L.E. 1974/1975 Developmental phases of encounter groups and related intensive groups. *Interpersonal Development, 5,* 112–129.

Garland, J. A., Jones, H. E., & Kolodny, R. L. (1976). A model for stages of development in social work groups. In S. Bernstein (Ed.), *Explorations in group work: Essays in theory and practice.* Boston: Charles River Books. pp. 17–71.

Johnson, C. (1974). Planning for termination of the group. In P. Glasser, R. Sarri, & R. Vinter (Eds.), *Individual change through small groups.* New York: Free Press. pp. 258–265.

Levine, B. (1967). *Fundamentals of group treatment.* Chicago: Whitehall.

Levine, B. (1979). *Group psychotherapy practice and development.* Englewood Cliffs, NJ: Prentice-Hall.

Mahler, M. S. (1968). *On human symbiosis and the vicissitudes of individuation.* New York: International Universities Press.

Pine, F. (1971). On the separation process: Universal trends and individual differences. In J. B. McDevitt & C. T. Settlage (Eds.), *Separation-individuation.* New York: International Universities Press. pp.113–130.

Rose, S. D. (1972). *Treating children in groups: A behavioral approach.* San Francisco: Jossey-Bass.

Scheidlinger, S. (1974). On the concept of the "mother-group." *International Journal of Group Psychotherapy, 24,* 417–428.

Slavson, S. R., & Schiffer, M. (1975). *Group psychotherapies for children.* New York: International Universities Press.

Trafimow, E., & Pattak, S. I. (1981). Group psychotherapy and objectal development in children. *International Journal of Group Psychotherapy, 31,* 193–204.

Yalom, I. D. (1970). *The theory and practice of group psychotherapy.* New York: Basic Books.

Chapter 8

STAGE VI: CLOSURE

Barbara B. Siepker

EXPERIENTIAL DESCRIPTION

With the closing of the doors and the final good-byes of the last session a hollow echo begins to resound in the halls. The children have departed and gone their separate ways. Some have been wildly demonstrative with promises of calling or writing; others have slipped away virtually unnoticed. The therapist moves alone from room to room, mingling with people in an attempt to escape the internal emptiness. It has indeed ended. That which was so tumultuous and elusive has slipped away, leaving its impression on all. The children and therapist are similarly affected. At times it feels as if a burdensome load has been lifted, as if everyone involved is elated to have more time, new beginnings, and new joys. Underneath there is an emptiness and profound awareness of the necessity to deal with this alone—the pain of losing one another and all that has been shared. Present is an aura of quiet individuality, sparked with an added strength that aids in handling these feelings. It is as if someone out there understands how hard it is to "go it alone."

Friends and relatives seem intuitively to sense this emptiness and offer caring and support. The life of the group goes on in memory. Some need to deny its importance, whereas others lose themselves in almost manic, obsessive behaviors. Still others show open sadness, grieving, and depression. This is a period of memories and reveries about experiences, together with nostalgia about the day and hour the group occurred. There is a need to fill the time, substituting something pleasant to help fill the emptiness. Everyone involved is changed; what has happened will always retain its impression. For the children there is the excitement and anticipation of being able to manage on one's own with new friendships and experiences. "What will I be doing a year from now?" "It's fun and exciting."

The therapist, most readily available for observation, now takes his turn at withdrawing and mulling over his experiences. This is his time to finish his good-bye to the group in his own way. He has been unable to complete his separation partially because of his concerns with everyone else's feelings and needs. Now that it is his chance, he periodically indulges himself in memories, searching for answers. "Will they be able to maintain their gains?" "What changes really did occur and why?" "Do they miss the group?" "Will their families allow them to maintain their gains?" "What do their teachers need to know in order to accept and manage them?" "What will become of them when they grow up?" "Will they have memories of the group?" "What is the real impact of this experience on us all?" The therapist is surprised to find himself experiencing intense feelings of pain and loss. "I have trouble concentrating." "I am absent-minded and and have managed to misplace my keys." "I was embarrassed when I choked as I started to talk about the group." He sometimes finds himself dreaming about the group or individual children. It sometimes takes a long time to complete his post-conference, follow-ups, reports, and final closures.

Less is known directly from the child concerning his experiences and feelings now that the group has ended. Usually extremes of behavior tend to come to the therapist's attention. A parent calls because he does not know how to handle a child's worsening behavior, or a school checks to find out what happened in the group because "he's a different child," or "he's worse than he ever was." As the final sessions ends, the child has thoroughly checked out whether it is okay to call, write, or visit the therapist for social or for more pressing reasons. Frequently, pleasant associations are made by the child as he recognizes familiar landmarks enroute to the agency, takes the same bus, passes by the agency, or hears it mentioned on TV or by friends. Pleasant memories remain, and the child may speak with pride about when he was "in that group at the clinic." For some children the experience is largely forgotten except for a positive feeling that groups and agencies can be helpful. For still others there is repression regarding ever having been in a group.

Children are very frequently heard from directly or by word of mouth. For older, more mobile children, there is "dropping by to visit" with the receptionist, secretary, or therapist, or "accidentally bumping into" them on the street. Cards, letters, and phone calls may be received, but more often news arrives via the grapevine. Occasionally the children themselves will arrange meetings with one another, especially when they have had previous contact outside of the group or when their parents have had contact with one another during the course of the group.

Concurrently, the parents are having mixed feelings accepting back the complete responsibility regarding their child's actions. They have depended on the therapist's help and frequently fear the child will begin to exhibit old symptoms that will trigger a chain of regressions. They almost panic when an old behavior occurs, questioning, "Is it all right for him to do this?" "What does it mean?" "Will he lose all of his gains?" "Will he be able to talk to me about it and will I be able to handle it alone?" "If we have to come back, does that mean he's been a failure?" "Maybe I should get him enrolled in a community group as suggested." There is a thrill or pride in their child's accomplishments and relief that their lives no longer need to be planned around the group's time. They look forward to increasingly satisfying relationships with their child and for him with other children. Some having seen the child's success, desire it for themselves and plan to enter treatment to achieve it.

The agency returns to old routines. No more friendly, jovial faces arrive an hour early to share their stories with the receptionist. It is almost as if the group has been forgotten except for references and comparisons to that "good old group" creeping into conversations. "There never was a group like that one!" "They would run through the halls and crawl under the furniture." "Remember when two of them ran out of the group room and locked themselves in the bathroom? Their pursuing therapist, returning empty-handed, turned purple when he found the group room locked!" "Finger painting was a disaster that day it became accidentally smudged all over the furniture, floors and walls and took two hours to clean up. The director really put his foot down then!" "Somehow we all survived." "It wasn't so bad after all." "I wonder when we'll have another one?" "Who will run this one?"

New groups reflect remnants of the old, echoing how it happened then and what changes should occur. The "old group therapist" becomes "expert consultant" and is looked to formally or informally for advice and support. Children contacted for new groups refer to their old groups. "My group therapist was really nice." "You mean we'll get to play where before we only talked?" Parents wonder why this group leader seems to advocate less freedom and more responsibilities. "How does this activity group compare to the other treatment group?" "Who will be in this group?" And so, gradually, everyone becomes immersed in the plans and recruiting for "the new group."

DYNAMIC DESCRIPTION

Although the *closure stage* is not recognized or conceptualized in the field as a stage of group treatment, it is an integral stage of treatment, especially with children and adolescents. Frequently due to this lack of recognition, stage VI is not expected or adequately prepared for by therapists. For some of the same reasons our stage model began before the first session it is extended beyond the last. Relationships, with their associated affects and memories, continue a life of their own within the human mind. Literature does not address itself beyond the last group session to the issues of terminating the relationships that have developed during the course of treatment. Garland, Jones, and Kolodny (1976) alert practitioners to the fact that intense feelings have developed in group relationships and that recognition needs to be given to their seriousness and how this affects termination. They note the phenomenon of children returning following groups and the possible need for continuing support as a part of the group worker's commitment.

The beginning of stage VI is the ending of the last session, lasts a few weeks to a number of months, and is largely influenced by the internal needs of the individual therapist to complete his or her work and the external demands of the agency. In another sense the reevaluation and memories of the group live on indefinitely. The stage formally ends with the inception of the idea of running a new group.

On closer examination the processes can be divided into three phases, which may vary slightly depending on idiosyncratic methods of handling separations. These phases are "letting go" of the group, "letting go" of the individuals, and reevaluation and preparation for a new group—the first two being rather abstract theoretical concepts recognized by and perhaps more useful to the introspective, conceptual-oriented therapist.

As the group in actuality no longer exists, phase one is letting go of the psychic construct of "the group" and its attendant meanings and feelings to the therapist, child, parent, and agency. This letting go incurs a process of separation and mourning for the total gestalt and phenomena of the group, involving global affects and identifications that are not unlike those made with familial, cultural, and societal groupings. These evolve with the passage of time. There is an acceptance of and comfort with this internalized identification with the therapy group that occurs in reminiscence and is accompanied by affects that resemble paternal, maternal, fraternal, and nationalistic feelings.

Phase two is a letting go of the individual children, parents, and therapist, necessitating a different level of separation, loss, and mourning. The "narcissistic tentacles" of intense interpersonal relationships must necessarily be removed from one another and returned to the individuals to allow separation and growth. For the child, the process results in identifications with and internalizations of the lost therapist and children. For the parent, the process includes identification with and trust in the therapist's conviction that the child is ready for termination and, it is hoped, an internalization of the therapist's ability to handle the anxiety and problems of the child. For the therapist, a personal loss of the children and his investments in them resolves itself through a process of identifying with the strengths, successes, and accomplishments of the child and parent. As the therapist has accepted that the children are ready for independent functioning, the dependent therapeutic relationship therefore is no longer necessary. The therapist receives satisfaction, gratification, and pride in a "job well done." This process is similar to a parent's healthy ability to allow the child to grow up, away and beyond them, yet remain comfortable in the knowledge they have contributed significantly and successfully to the child's development. They can allow the child to take credit for his own accomplishment and growth but remain available if needed.

Delays in the process of letting go of individual children occur when children need additional treatment or management following the group. Children are either referred or are seen by the group therapist. In either case the therapist will need to let go, in relationship to the group treatment aspects, and new therapeutic contracts will need to be negotiated. There is closure on the group portion of the relationship. Adequate completion of these feelings can allow the child, parent, and therapist to move beyond the group into new experiences. This process is generally considered completed when post-conferences, follow-ups, reports, and agency requirements are completed.

The ongoing process of reevaluation, putting into perspective the whole experience of group therapy as exemplified by "this group," and preparation for new groups, are the highlights of phase three. This is largely the task of the therapist, although frequently agencies assist in this by planning evaluation conferences. Another level of conceptualization and cognitive understanding takes place gradually through retrospective thinking, discussion, presentation, reading, and consultation around this group experience and group therapy more generally. As this process progresses, the therapist becomes aware of a growing, nagging desire to try another group in order to have more comparisons, challenges, and experiences. Conceptualizations begin to occur about this new group in which new ideas and techniques will be applied and further tested.

The Child

The child's separation was largely completed during the termination stage. Information regarding what happens to the child following the last session is most often incomplete and conjectured. A child's response to separation varies widely, depending on the child's ego functioning, ability to verbalize internal processes, personality patterns in handling feelings, the quality of parent-child relationship, progress within the group, and previous reactions to losses. Most of these responses were clearly demonstrated in stage V. Significant therapeutic gains during the group allowed the child to achieve an appropriate developmental stage. It is assumed the child adequately handles any remaining feelings and issues with his or her parents and friends. What significant influences the therapist and group continue to have on the child lies within the theoretical realm of identifications and internalizations. These cannot be measured or observed directly, even if the child were more available for comment.

Children who from all indications have teminated successfully will sometimes return as a matter of checking in with the therapist to receive recognition and acceptance for his or her new accomplishments. These contacts are best handled neutrally, in a friendly, relatively nontherapeutic manner, rather than encouraging a reinvestment or reestablishment of a prior intense relationship. The child needs to know the therapist enjoys seeing him, remembers him, and continues to remain available at the agency. These contacts are best made at the child's initiation. The therapist can appropriately initiate contact regarding the child by checking *on* the child and his progress through contacting parents, schools, and agencies, rather than directly *with* the child.

Children who experienced greater difficulty terminating and progressing through the stages will sometimes need direct contact with the therapist in addition to their parents, school or community. In most cases these are the children who have a history of separation problems. These children can be identified by their increase in symptoms, parents' and teacher's alarm, which may occur within days of the final session. Unable to complete their separations, these children are still dependent on the therapist for understanding and interpretation. Other children also suppress closing off in terms of the group experience, especially the pain of separation, and may withdraw and cut themselves off from their feelings. Children having transitional difficulties will need more support from their environment in order to use this stage to complete their termination. These children need to see the therapist a few times, to assure his or her continued availability. A relationship may need to continue until the child is able to let go and be transferred to another group or individual therapist.

The Therapist

The process of separation can be studied and observed most directly in the therapist. As much as he feels he recognized and handled his feelings during the termination stage, he was busy "holding the group together" through dissolution and did not have a great deal of time, energy, or distance with which to handle his own. The novice therapist is sometimes unpleasantly surprised and unprepared for dealing with the intensity and impact of his feelings during the closure stage. He had expected all to be over with the last session, even though he secretly feared all would return the following week with the same problems. He questions whether he should have such strong feelings. Even experienced therapists are sometimes surprised at their intensity. The therapist has invested a great deal of himself, received a lot in return, and needs to feel the treatment has been successful. He would like to protect his investment by "turning the child over to capable and loving hands," the ideal solution, or at least find a reasonable compromise. He is wary of turning over "his group of children" to insensitive but well-meaning, or sensitive but sabotaging, parents or teachers. He would like to ensure that accomplished gains will be maintained and that continued growth is possible.

Recognizing and handling his own separation process involves the therapist's accepting the finality that the child is no longer externally influenced by the therapist. The responsibility for the therapy has ended, and only an administrative, semitherapeutic one remains for transfer, disposition, and closure. To separate emotionally necessitates balancing his feelings of power, authority, omnipotence, and grandiosity with worthlessness, self-depreciation, powerlessness, and helplessness. Experiencing a mixture, he eventually ends up feeling somewhere in the middle. "Significant progress was made in these specific areas, but not these for the following reasons . . ." "A combination of these factors resulted in this change . . ."

The natural course of the passage of time is a crucial factor in the separation process. The separation from "the group" as an entity requires that the therapist come to terms with the mixed feelings encompassed in and resulting from the overall group experience. Although the stages have been discussed with clarity as they progressed, the impact of their entirety at times seems overwhelming. As each group varies so much in overall flow and intensity, certain stages stand out dramatically. Certain of these may loom out of proportion, taking on almost living characterizations. Most likely these are shared good-naturedly with a colleague or consultant. Sometimes they are experienced more seriously within, revolving around conflictual issues for the therapist. Sometimes denied or ignored, they wait and may nag for a chance at restitution. Optimally, the therapist has help emerging from this scenario with resolution or at very least with motivation and goals to try it again with certain differences and modifications. For some groups, the fact they made it through all or even some of the stages intact is indeed an accomplishment worthy of appreciation. Each group has its own set of accompanying memories, living on in the thoughts of the therapist, children, parents, and agency.

At group's end the therapist's investment is still active in regard to each child. Contracts, goals, and therapeutic progress is reevaluated for each child. The therapist's goal and work is to ensure successful transition to home, school, and community. Because of this he finds himself wanting to reassure significant others that the child is really sensitive, bright, perceptive, and caring even though the child may defend against this, show the opposite, or have trouble expressing himself well. The therapist often is reassuring himself and alleviating anxiety regarding the child's improvement. There also will be warnings regarding the child's behavior, such as when anxious or angry he will need distance or a chance to withdraw temporarily. There is the nagging impression of unfinished business until he assures himself that each child made a successful bridge from the group and himself back to the outside world.

Concurrent reevaluation has been occurring, determining whether goals have been accomplished. This process becomes final with post-conferences, follow-ups, treatment summaries, and agency reports and can take weeks or months to complete. The manner and time in which these are completed reflect both the idiosyncrasies of the therapist and the state of his resolving the separation. In the process the therapist separates from the children first singularly and then collectively. In his memory they remain individualized and the group distinctive.

The final step is to conceptualize and integrate this group's process and stages as compared with other groups the therapist has knowledge of or led. This includes recognition and acceptance of the feelings generated by this group. The therapist evaluates his professional and personal standing as affected by this group.

Therapists should continue to consult with their supervisors for a session or more past the group's termination to help put the experience into perspective. The consultative relationship must be brought to closure to facilitate their moving into a similar relationship with a new group or moving into a co-therapy or colleague role.

When co-therapists exist, this phase involves letting go of their reciprocal group relationship. Putting closure on this group's experiences will allow their relationship to enter into a new dimension, which might include co-therapy with another group.

For the therapist who has been able to understand, accept, and put these intense feelings into perspective, comes professional contentment. With more time and less external bombardment, considerable retrospective assessment can be accomplished. Ironically, much of the conceptualizing and understanding of the group and the individual process occurs in retrospect, especially for the novice therapist. He may often search the group literature for further understanding. He has not always been pleased by his feelings and reactions. He has come to know the primitive feelings and anxieties aroused by the group, of the internal and external boundaries of his anger, anxiety, caring, and sensitivity, and is more sure about those he can handle easily and those causing him anxiety and difficulty. Putting closure on the group allows him to think about a future group and the changes he will make.

The Parents

Parents, for many of their own reasons, are not always able to or do not wish to carry through on recommendations given during the termination stage. This is a frustrating experience for an invested therapist, even though these cases are usually predictable. When the parent fails to carry through on recommendations or refuses treatment for his or her child the therapist has few and often inconclusive options. He can attempt to mobilize the parent to follow through by scheduling appointments with him or her to review the progress, stressing the importance of further care for the child, and by informing the referring source of the family's failure to follow through so that further persuasion may be applied. If these approaches do not bring the results hoped for, there are only two remaining choices. He can give up and allow the parent the autonomy of his decision, coming to peace with the fact that as much outside therapeutic influence as is possible has been provided currently for child. If it is a case of extreme, provable neglect—not providing necessary psychiatric care, or abuse—the only choice is to report to the proper authority or attempt a legal suit to get the indicated care or placement for the child. The latter cases are few but worth the effort when one's ethical and professional motivations are sufficiently aroused regarding the child's welfare and future.

The Agency

During stage VI most agencies set a structure, at best also supportive, for the therapist to work through his or her separation following the group's ending. By expecting treatment summaries the agency is providing the necessity and the vehicle through which the therapist can utilize his or her intellectual capacities to pull together and evaluate the progress a child and the group have made. Useful conceptualization takes place through review, helping put the experience into perspective and one step away from the experiential.

Deadlines for report writing and case closures are often instigated by the agency not only to meet their deadlines but to help the therapist mobilize himself around the work of separation. In a sense these deadlines are self-imposed limits set by administrators who have been through this before and found them helpful. Therapists react to deadlines with varying patterns of compliance, rebellion, compulsivity, avoidance, and procrastination, all of which are frequently accompanied by anger and guilt for not having done the work earlier.

Clinical treatment summaries are crucial means of communicating to agencies and schools. These cover the areas of strengths, weaknesses, changes a child has made, further work needed, and useful techniques in handling the child, especially his or her difficult behaviors. The clinical summary often begins, stimulates, or ends the therapist's process of reevaluation. This process, as already stated, is crucial to the therapist's handling of his feeings of separation. It allows the therapist the necessary distancing from his clinical experience with the child and group and continues to pave the way for a more objective perspective of observing rather than directly experiencing. This is accomplished because the therapist must look back at what has been experienced, compare with prior symptoms, behavior, and age-appropriate cultural norms, and draw certain impressions and conclusions as to the child's current functioning. The therapist is then further pushed by this process to speculate why the changes occurred and the function and nature of the improvements. The reevaluative process is taking place, which is a healthy part of allowing a therapist to gain emotional distance. Treatment summaries are often followed by treatment staffings to present an overview of the treatment progression and to formalize decisions, recommendations, and dispositions.

In addition to clinical reporting therapists often are encouraged by their agencies to formulate the broader implications of their experiences with the group as a whole in the form of group process treatment staffings, conferences, didactics, and seminars, which often have the goal of evaluating a group's experience and providing a teaching experience. This provides a chance to make statements about group treatment and for the agency staff to familiarize themselves further with group process and stages of treatment. It is hoped that all of these will culminate in the happy conclusion that psychotherapeutic groups with children can be survived and enjoyed.

SPECIAL ISSUES

Handling Separation

Looking again at the entire stage, it is clear that for all parties involved the overriding process begun in stage V is an internal one of experiencing separation and mourning. The individual's handling of this phenomenon is clinically, experientially, and theoretically accepted and understood to be influenced and patterned after all previous separations and losses. Separation is usually experienced as a complex, difficult process involving intense feelings that arise and quickly are covered over and defended against because of discomfort, pain, and a fear of being overwhelmed. Experienced are sadness, anger, and emptiness.

Separation and mourning are universal phenomena that can resolve themselves in healthy, active ways or more pathological ways. By the closure stage, the process is already fully begun, with healthy resolution hinging on acceptance, a necessity of time, and letting it proceed along its natural course. The internal processes brought to play more frequently in healthy resolution are identifying with aspects of the lost object, sharing feelings with the lost object, or projecting their mutuality onto the lost object, and discussing with others in an effort to share, reminisce, and gain an intellectual and conceptual perspective. Observable is a movement and dynamic interplay between loss of the object and pleasure of therapeutic gain. There is typically no need for contact or intervention during this healthy process.

It is sometimes difficult to imagine how an adult can allow a child to separate and proceed with the lifelong process of growing into adulthood. The joys and gratifications an adult receives vicariously by reliving childhood through children has many satisfactions. There is always present the wishful, magical thinking that allows the therapist, parent, and child to feel "this can and should go on forever." It is easy to find a need and a reason to continue treatment and hard to find a reason to terminate, especially when the child is from a chaotic, rejecting, or pathological home. To help a child with the realities of life, to let him or her face the world alone, not yet totally prepared, indeed feels at times cruel and unnecessary. There never is an "ideal" time, solution, or place to refer a child. There remains for the adult an unfulfilled wish to see the child through the completion of childhood with all of its incumbent tasks and gratifications. If therapy has been working well for this child, there's a wish to prolong and enjoy it. If a child is moving slowly or not at all, there is both a wish to quit and a need to continue in hopes of treatment accelerating. The therapist must come to grips with the group's being but "for a moment" in this child's life and learn to be comfortable letting the child go on to experience the many relationships, tasks, joys, and hardships remaining in that fluid state called childhood. This necessitates trusting that the child has internalized something useful to him and that future adults will look on the child favorably, offering support as needed.

Theory remains inconclusive as to the degree and influence of mourning in the young child. The type and extent of a loss experience may be quantitatively and qualitatively different from that of an adult as well as perhaps being less lengthy or elaborate. Age, ego functioning, and dynamics of disturbance are factors in this process. The younger the child, or the less able he or she is to conceptualize and function with an observing ego, the more difficulty he will have in understanding and handling the separation. For those who have not reached the stage of separation-individuation, the experience of loss may be more for lost parts of self. Some experience an actual loss of an object; others will experience a loss of love from a significant object. For an older child who also possesses stronger ego functioning and more independence, the experience can result in a solid identification with and internalization of functioning gained through the therapist and the group. Identifications begun during the group continue and often expand in fantasy. The loss experience for this child may be more of losing former aspects of himself such as his symptomatic behavior patterns.

The more unusual and exceptional cases of incomplete, unresolved, or acute mourning are more blatant and in need of special attention. The therapist must intervene and work with the child or parent around the block or inhibition to the normal processes of mourning. Unresolved mourning is evident when the following continue past interpretation: the fantasy wish to "remain together forever," anxiety or obsession regarding the transfer arrangements, denial of the continued existence of problems through an omnipotent incorporation, or a global regression to earlier, more regressed, symptomatic functioning. An aura of fixity and rigidity prevails, indicative of unresolved, sealed-over conflicts. Acute suffering and pain indicate an inability to accept the loss, possibly due to previous unaccepted losses. When evidence is not present of active mourning, one is alerted to the probability of suppressed, unresolved mourning.

The technique or manner in which the therapist intervenes is largely dependent on the child's or parents' prior patterns and the therapist's orientation. In one case, the therapist may be supportive, accepting, and understanding of the intense, endless pain and help the child recognize its genetic and dynamic roots, or in another case the therapist may help the child make a decision to "give up" the inappropriateness of the feelings and the endless, overwhelming burden these create. The important common denominator is to confront the separation problem by focusing attention on it, discussing it with and interpreting it to the child and/or his family, and working with them until some resolution can be achieved so that the child can be free to move on to investing in new relationships.

Children *do* frequently return to the therapist's attention in one way or another for visits or follow-up care. Their return does not necessarily reflect on the validity or integrity of group therapy, the therapist's skill or countertransference, or resolution of the child's problems. Termination is often conceptualized in child therapy more as an interruption in treatment rather than completion, as in an adult model. Often child treatment has as its goal to return or bring the child up to an age-appropriate stage of development. The tasks and conflicts of later stages of development are still ahead for the child and may cause him or her future difficulties necessitating additional support or treatment.

Not all therapists are equally successful in handling their separation feelings. Some exhibit depression, obsession, or manic behavior, whereas others withdraw and rely on previously confirmed attitudes about themselves as therapists. These may be extreme, rigidly held conceptualizations. Some therapists overestimate their effectiveness and importance, which frequently covers underlying issues of self-doubt. They have trouble accepting that someone else can love and handle a child as well as they can, which results in their remaining overinvolved, unable to allow separation. Therapist inadequacy and insecurity also may be evident in criticism of his role in the group or depreciation of the contributions of home, school, and community in the changes a child has experienced. Anxiety surrounding his professional or therapeutic contribution may cause him to be excessively concerned regarding the expertise and professionalism of the help or treatment that is to follow. For some therapists this is a trying stage, sometimes never completed. Parcels of feelings, loss, overinvolvement, and failure are carried around. These do not allow him to have another group because of vulnerability and inability to work these feelings through. Ideally, therapists with difficulties in resolving their mourning will be picked up by supervisors and consultants in discussion, staffings, or group presentations, or will be self-identified. Mourning needs to progress in order for the therapist to remove his or her investment in the children and to allow a final separation. Only then can the child be free to invest elsewhere and the therapist free to consider undertaking other group therapy experiences.

Signs of Successful Treatment

Successes in treatment are largely seen and judged through the eyes of the "beholder." The therapist who formulated goals for the child feels successful if these have been achieved. Children, their parents, and teachers have also set goals they hoped would be accomplished. The parent or teacher who was irritated by a certain symptom is relieved when this has disappeared and annoyed if it remains. The parent who wants happiness for his child will be pleased when he no longer seems driven with behavior and conflict and seems to enjoy life. The rewards of successful treatment are often fed back to the therapist through pleased children, parents, and teachers in the form of thanks, visits, praise, or more referrals.

Handling Terminations and Transfers

When the child transfers to another therapist within the agency or to another agency, any contact with the therapist should support the child's new treatment. When the child is ambivalent regarding the transfer and uses this to try to engage the group therapist into siding with his negative feelings, the therapist must be wary and hold a consistent, neutral position regarding their relationship while encouraging the child to bring his feelings to his current therapist to work them out. The therapist can support this by reviewing with the child their beginning relationship, when the child felt similarly toward him but ended up feeling very positively. The therapist shows his caring through demonstration that he wants the child to get something from his new treatment relationship. This is not the time or place for strong, mixed feelings the therapist may have regarding the new therapist or agency. These ambivalent feelings should have been handled prior to making the transfer. The child must be set free to form a new therapeutic alliance. Although transfers in treatment are indeed difficult and often less than ideal, they are virtually impossible when the ambivalent therapist is unable to allow and help the child to separate from him.

Dropouts that have occurred much earlier in the group life are handled much better at the time they occur so that appropriate dispositions can be made. If this was not done at that time and the child returns after the group's termination, an assessment needs to be made to determine what service the child and his family are seeking and ready to invest in, as well as what is therapeutically indicated at this time. It is preferrable for this assessment to be done by the group therapist if he has the time and experience necessary. If not, a referral should be made.

There are definable limits to the therapist's responsibility regarding transfer and disposition of cases. Given the inherent limitations of ideal therapeutic milieus in which to transfer a child, the therapist must make the most educated, realistic, yet therapeutic decision regarding disposition. At the same time he needs to come to grips with his own narcissism and grandiosity that he is the best or only person who can really understand and help this child. Once he has been able to rcognize and accept the limitations in choosing an ideal situation and has come to internal peace regarding his helpfulness and effectiveness with a child, he will be able gradually to decrease his investments and allow successful separation of the children. Not until this is complete and the therapist is finally satisfied that every child in his group has been "properly transferred" can he complete his mourning.

REFERENCE

Garland, J. A., Jones, H. E., & Kolodny, R. L. (1976). A model of development in social work groups. In S. Bernstein (Ed.), *Explorations in group work: Essays in theory and practice*. Boston: Charles River Books. pp. 17-71.